KU-260-003

Law in Society Series

KNOWLEDGE AND
OPINION ABOUT LAW

Knowledge and Opinion about Law

ADAM PODGORECKI, WOLFGANG KAUPEN,
J. VAN HOUTTE, P. VINKE, BERL KUTCHINSKY

Law in Society Series

edited by
C. M. CAMPBELL, W. G. CARSON, P. N. P. WILES

MARTIN ROBERTSON

© *Attitudes Governing the Acceptance of Legislation* J. Van Houtte and P. Vinke 1973; © *Public Opinions of the Law* W. Kaupen 1973; © *Public Opinion on Law* A. Podgorecki 1973; *The Legal Consciousness* B. Kutchinsky 1973.

All rights reserved. No part of this publication may be reproduced, stored in a retrieval system, or transmitted in any form or by any means, electronic, mechanical, photocopying, recording or otherwise, without the prior written permission of the copyright holder.

First published in 1973 by Martin Robertson and Company Ltd, 17 Quick Street, London N1 8HL.

ISBN 0 85520 017 0

Printed in Great Britain by
The Barleyman Press, Bristol

CONTENTS

INTRODUCTORY NOTE

Writing of the way in which law, by giving recognition to ideals, plays comforter as well as guide to the community, Thurman Arnold has observed that 'the principles of law are supposed to control society, because such an assumption is necessary to the logic of the dream'. If law is regarded simply as an abstract deductive system or as a pragmatic exercise to be appraised purely in its own terms, the gap between such dreams and the reality need be of little consequence. But within the context of the sociology of law which adopts a different interpretive framework and utilizes rather different criteria, such a circumscribed approach can never be wholly satisfactory. Like Arnold, the sociologist of law may interest himself in the wider social functions of the symbolic element in law; or, like those whose intrigue is with the gap between the law in books and the law in action, he may become preoccupied with the extent to which it actually achieves its social objectives. The latter issue has of course been one subject of long-standing interest, and moreover, promises to become one of the focal concerns for studies of law in society which are emerging in Britain at the present time. [Another monograph being published in this series under the title *Social Needs and Legal Action* is one example of this hopeful trend.]

But a sociologically oriented attempt to scrutinize legal assumptions more closely also raises other and no less basic questions. *Do* the principles of law control society? If they do, *how* is this effect actually achieved, regardless of the assumption's centrality to the ideals symbolized in law? While questions about the basis on which men accept authority have indeed occupied the minds of sociologists from Weber to Parsons, problems about how and to what extent legal percepts intrude into the exigencies of everyday life have been largely ignored. We may indeed be 'a nation of laws

7

and not of men', but ultimately it is the men who through their attitudinal stances, opinions, moral decisions and overt behaviour transform the assumed control function of law into a reality, if such it is.

In this volume, a number of eminent European scholars investigate one crucial dimension of this broader problem by focusing upon the knowledge and opinion of law prevailing in their culturally diverse societies, and by setting out the social correlates of the patterns which emerge. By this approach, they attempt to shed some light upon the degree to which assumptions about such nebulae as legal consciousness, legal sentiments and legal awareness can stand up to empirical scrutiny.

This does not mean however, that their basic stance is primarily iconoclastic. For in different ways, each of the contributors also recognizes that appeal is frequently made to the assumptions in question as yardsticks for establishing the validity, legitimacy and direction of law. Thus, in investigating the empirical bases of some legal presuppositions, they are also raising questions about equally important issues of legality and the appropriate criteria for the shaping of law. In Berl Kutchinsky's forceful phrase, they are concerned with 'the knowledge and opinion of those who are not only being controlled by the law, but who should also be the controllers of law'. While their conclusions in this respect may lead them in different and certainly debatable directions, this orientation is one which a sociology of law purporting to embrace not just *the rules of law* but also the *rule of law*, cannot afford to ignore.

In terms of its theoretical background, methodology and approach to problems of policy, the material in this book represents a tradition which has become established on the continent of Europe in recent decades. While it must therefore inevitably diverge in places from what the British reader finds familiar, or even appropriate, at a time when the sociology of law is beginning to emerge in this country, it is fitting that we should acquaint ourselves with the research which is going on elsewhere. From the work of these five scholars, preeminent in this field in their respective countries, there is much to be learned by those who may set out to tackle the somewhat neglected area of knowledge and opinion of law in Britain. In this connection perhaps the most distinctive feature of this collection is the way in which the authors
8

not only display their familiarity with each other's work, but also undertook their respective projects with the objective firmly in mind of developing substantially similar programmes. In consequence we find them borrowing ideas, strategies and techniques so freely from each other that cross-referencing becomes largely redundant. By their borrowing they both lay the foundations for comparative analysis in this field and provide us with an example from which the emerging sociology of law in this country might derive considerable benefit.

C.M.C.
W.G.C.
P.N.P.W.

NOTES ON THE AUTHORS

Adam Podgorecki has degrees in law and sociology from the Iagiellonian University, Krakow and Warsaw University where he has been Professor of Sociology since 1961. In recent years he was Visiting Professor at Northwestern University and Fellow at All Souls College, Oxford. This year he is Visiting Professor at the University of Pennsylvania, a National Science Foundation Fellow and continues to hold several senior posts in the International Sociological Association. He is author and co-author of many very influential books in the fields of sociology of law and socio-technics.

Wolfgang Kaupen, M.A., Dr. phil., studied law and sociology at the Universities of Cologne and Mannheim. He is a Fellow of the German Research Foundation, Director of the Cologne Working Group for Sociology of Law and is Lecturer for Sociology of Law at the Universities of Cologne and Regensburg.

His publications include two books, *Die Huter von Recht und Ordnung* (The Protectors of Law and Order: Socialization, Education, and Professional Training of the German Jurists), 1969, and (with Judge Theo Rasehorn) *Die Justiz zwischen Obrigkeitsstaat und Demokratie* (Justice between Authoritarian State and Democracy), 1971. Dr Kaupen's current research is a study of the functions of law as a mechanism of social control.

J. Van Houtte, doctor in law, M.A. in criminology, doctor in political and social sciences, is Professor in Sociology and Sociology of Law, Dean of the Faculty of Political and Social Sciences, University Faculties St Ignatius, and Director of the Centre for Sociology of Law at the University of Antwerp.

Apart from the research described in this volume he is studying

11

family law, particularly problems of maintenance, and has worked extensively in religious sociology and population and family problems. He has several publications in the sociology of religion and the sociology of law.

P. Vinke studied economics and tax-law and was for many years an inspector in the Dutch inland revenue service. Developing an interest in sociology he wrote a doctoral thesis on the social position and mobility of company directors and then in 1965 was appointed Professor of Tax-law and Fiscal Sociology at Leyden University. He is now Professor of Sociology of Law, and is a member of the board of the European Research Committee on Sociology of Law of the International Sociological Association. His current research is on the acceptance of legal rules.

Berl Kutchinsky was from 1962 to 1965 and from 1967 to 1970 a Research Fellow at the University of Copenhagen, affiliated with the Institute of Criminal Science. Since 1970 he has been a Research Assistant at the Institute of Criminal Science. In 1968 he became chairman of the international research group on Knowledge and Opinion About Law. In 1971 he was appointed a member of the Sub-Committee on Decriminalization under the Council of Europe, and between 1964 and 1969 he was Editor-in-Chief of the official journal of the Nordic Psychological Association *Nordisk Psykologi*. His thesis 'The General Sense of Justice' was published in 1970, 'The Perception of Deviance: A Survey of Empirical Research' is to be published by the Council of Europe, and his recent research is to be published in 1973 by Martin Robertson under the title 'Pornography and Sex Crimes in Denmark'.

ATTITUDES GOVERNING THE ACCEPTANCE OF LEGISLATION AMONG VARIOUS SOCIAL GROUPS

J. Van Houtte and P. Vinke

This article concerns some parts of an investigation performed by the Sociology of Law Department, Faculty of Law of the University of Leiden and a related study by the Centre for Sociology of Law, Academic Faculties St Ignatius, University of Antwerp. Participants in the Dutch study were C. J. M. Schuyt (who was succeeded by Mrs I. J. Berghuis-Van der Wijk) and J. C. M. Ruijs, who contributed to this paper. The investigation in the Netherlands was made possible by support from the Dutch Organization for the Advancement of Pure Scientific Research, and will be published in the near future by the Kluwer Publishing Company. In the Belgian investigation J. Lefevere also co-operated and contributions to the article were made by R. Lafaille and I. Callens. The results of the Belgian investigation will be published in the near future.

THE BACKGROUND OF RESEARCH ON THE ACCEPTANCE OF LEGAL RULES

The doctrine of human conviction as a basis for legal rules

Although several empirical studies on the acceptance of legal rules have been published fairly recently,[1] neither legal scholars nor sociologists have a clear picture of this empirical approach. We therefore wish to clarify the considerations which led us to undertake the study under discussion, and to sketch for the uninitiated reader the background against which the subject of the study must be seen.

The decision to undertake a study always has a personal element, and in this, our investigation is no exception, being based on an empirical study by Podgorecki.[2] Interest in the subject arose from a number of theories of, and perspectives on, law (including those of sociologists) as well as from the social relevance we see in an understanding of the preconditions for the acceptance or rejection of legal rules.

In a number of modern theories on law and views on the obligatory character of legal rules, we discerned and were intrigued by an unanswered question concerning the gap between the assumed basis of a law's legitimacy—individual conviction and social control—and the actual acceptance of the rule. The idea that the inner conviction of individuals with regards to a rule is of decisive importance for its legitimacy is found in the doctrine of 'the sense of justice' (*Rechtsgefühl, Rechtsbewusstsein*),[3] according to which no rule can bind a man except by his own conviction.[4] Krabbe, the Dutch proponent of this view who spoke from his humanistic religious belief, said that instead of the ancient gods—the public authority—we are presented with another authority—individual conscience or conviction—which has been internalized and in this form exercises more real power over us than was inherent in the concept of a more natural subserviency to Authorities presumably endowed with prestige. As we are now aware and as is becoming clearer every day, authority lies locked in our spiritual life.[5] A similar undertone of humanistic emancipation can be discerned in Fuller: 'To embark on the enterprise of subjecting human conduct to the governance of rules involves of necessity a commitment to the view that man is, or can become, a responsible agent, capable of understanding and following rules and answerable for his defaults.'[6] A similar longing for human emancipation is expressed by Selznick: 'a conception of law as the manifestation of awesome authority encourages feelings of deference and is compatible with much arbitrary rule. In a community that aspires to a high order of legality obedience to law is not submissive compliance. The obligation to obey the law is closely tied to the defensibility of the rules themselves and of the official decisions that enforce them'.[7]

These ideas lead us to the problem of how those for whom the laws are made actually perceive and accept them. A similar question is raised by the doctrine according to which the legitimacy of a law lies in the conviction of a group. 'What is important is that the insistence on importance or *seriousness* of social pressure behind the rules is the primary factor determining whether they are thought of as giving rise to obligations'.[8] Paralleling this we find in Dicey and in Sumner: (Dicey) 'The opinion which affects the development of the law has, in modern England at least, often originated with some single thinker or school of thinkers' and 'Laws foster or create law-making opinion'.[9] One of the most quoted passages in Sumner is: 'Legislation ... has to seek standing ground on the existing mores, and ... legislation to be strong must be consistent with the mores'.[10]

Both these ideas emerged partially at a time in which modern legislation characteristic of a welfare state was less well developed than it now is. But these ideas on modern legislation may be one-sided to a certain extent. The sense of justice (Krabbe), the responsibility and the capacity to understand and follow rules (Fuller), or the defensibility of the rules themselves (Selznick), may be weaker as a basis of legitimacy for modern legislation than for older legislation with its roots in tradition. Furthermore, factors such as self-interest, lack of comprehension and friction in administration, can strongly influence attitudes to modern laws. Nonetheless, empirical research on the gap between a sense of justice and social control as basic factors in the legitimacy of a rule or the acceptance of that rule within the framework of reality, is imperative for the understanding of rules of law.

All this led us to the study of attitudinal differences between countries, and between social groups, in various areas of law-making.

The social relevance of information concerning the acceptance of rules of law in various social groups

This point also seemed to us to warrant research. Having described what ought to happen, the study of law rarely proceeds to the description of what actually happens and, in consequence, it is not surprising that the question of the acceptance of legal rules has remained beyond the horizon. The matrix of thinking in doctrines of law is so specific that any combination with an empirical approach is far from simple. Indeed, the difference in thinking underlying the normative and empirical approaches emphasizes

15

their divergence[11] even though their combination would promote a less fragmentary consideration of legal rules.

It is also true that in a rather uncomplicated pre-industrial society the need for empirical research was less pressing than it is for present-day society, and there was little reason for jurisprudence to concern itself with the empirical reality of law. *Mutatis mutandis* the same holds for sociology.

Our own study was not entirely immune from this anaemia which has characterized sociological and jurisprudential contributions to the empirical approach to law. When a theoretical model corresponding to reality is lacking,[12] a study of what actually happens in the context of law must necessarily start by being descriptive and by adopting hypotheses which represent only a small link in the chain of theory formation.

In connection with this report it is hoped that the reader will accept the words of Romain Rolland that '*Il faut aimer la vérité plus que soi-même, mais son prochain plus que la vérité*'[13] and not only see the writer as his *prochain* but also accept that all he has at his disposal is a poor theoretical tool.

Although practical know-how, a sociology of law *avant la lettre*, was sufficient for observations on the acceptance of legal rules in a pre-industrial society, this is clearly no longer the case. Our times demand that jurisprudence should have the sociological imagination[14] to realize the extent to which social changes in tempo and in values[15] in the social groups involved, have fundamentally changed the social milieu of our law. Investigation into attitudes towards legislation can contribute to a clearer understanding of that milieu. This understanding becomes increasingly important when, for the ultimate legitimation of legal rules in a society, it becomes less and less possible to resort to the teachings of philosophy and theology.[16] Philosophy of law must become more and more modest in its claims, just as religion now tends to shrink back from many subjects about which it would once have pronounced decisive judgements.[17]

This does not mean that the results of empirical investigation into the acceptance of legal rules can be expected to decide what law should be.[18] But in the long run this kind of research can supply information about a series of facts relevant for jurisprudence, facts which might seem to indicate that a law should be considered obsolete, that submissive compliance is involved, that a law is not

16

comprehended, and that informal codes underly a formal rule. The legislation that regulated individual *do ut des* relationships and individual criminality in the traditional sense had much less reason to consider an inherent system of acceptance than does legislation falling in the collective sphere—labour laws, market control and fiscal rules. Although the latter types of legislation affect the daily interests of large groups of people, it is quite conceivable that they are vulnerable at crucial points, partially as a result of lack of acceptance by various groups. It is indeed valid to ask: 'How much of the original objective of government by popular consent can be sustained in a system in which the sphere of active government has been greatly enlarged and is likely to become more so?'[19]

This remains a relevant question in a period of almost unbounded optimism[20] born of full employment and high investment previously unknown in Europe.[21] It will certainly also be a pressing question in a period, perhaps soon to come, when our society will be faced with restrictive distribution of facilities and limitation of freedom of choice in social behaviour. As a result of all these considerations, an investigation into the acceptance of legal rules seemed to us the proper way to begin our work in the field of the sociology of law.[22]

THE SUBJECT OF THE INVESTIGATION

Hypotheses to be verified by the investigation

Industrialization has meant that in our society social behaviour is to a high degree determined by secondary relationships[23] on organizational levels (macro and middle range levels). The traditional organizations responsible for management, the solution of conflicts and education have proliferated, while new structures have arisen for the development of industry and for the regulation of traffic, social security, regional planning and the like. The huge modern corporations, the new population agglomerations and the communication media have led to impersonal group formation with unprecedented dimensions and complexity.

The penetration of these relationships into the pattern of social behaviour is reflected in the innumerable asymmetrical legal rela-

17

tionships occurring in our society today. By this we mean the unequal relationships in which collective agents have much more power than individuals. These relationships are mainly the result of legislation in which the state manifests itself as protector, dispenser of social resources, industrial manager, and economic controller and arbitrator.[24] Such relational disparities are also produced by standard contracts, vertical price agreements and by other forms of regulation which oligopoloid market positions make possible for a number of entrepreneurs.

Thus, our subject must now be seen against the background of the many legislative rules and contracts in the collective sphere which put responsibilities on the individual or give him rights without consulting him. It is conceivable that the prevalence of laws in which the interests of a collectivity or of a particular organization rather than the interests of individuals[25] are supported—i.e. legislation in the socio-economic sphere—tends to 'patterned evasion'[26] through the development of informal codes of conduct.

It may be assumed that various factors such as obscurity of the contribution to the collective purpose of the rule, limited comprehension of the collective purpose in question, and divergence between the individual and the collective interest exert an influence on the degree to which rules of law are accepted. In approaching our subject we were compelled to restrict ourselves to an attempt to verify two hypotheses:

1. With respect to various rules of law in the collective sphere, the population has highly divergent attitudes.
2. The difference in attitude toward various types of legal rules is related to socio-structural, socio-cultural, and psychological factors.

Methodology

For the verification of these hypotheses it was necessary to have data representative of the entire population and permitting a high degree of quantification and generalization with adequate precision, completeness and efficiency. In our opinion, the survey method[27] is consistent with these criteria. Comprising questions on the respondent's attitude towards certain legal rules the question-

18

naire used in this survey focused on attitudes underlying manifest behaviour[28] rather than on the behaviour itself. It thus provides only a partial measure of acceptance. The same would have been true if we had limited ourselves to a behavioural study since observation of behaviour in relation to a rule only illuminates the external factors involved in acceptance (fear of sanctions and/or social control) and not the internal factors towards which an attitude study is oriented. Public opinion in the sense of the attitudes prevailing among different parts of the public,[29] i.e. groups with divergent social characteristics constituting dependent variables in our study, form a socially distinguishable empirical datum indicating the place taken by a norm in subjective feelings about law.

The Belgian part of the survey comprised 460 interviewees, based on a stratified sample of the occupied male population of the conurbation of Antwerp, and for the Dutch part, 1,087 interviewees (raised to 1,300 for the statistical analysis) on the basis of a representative sample of the gainfully employed population (male and female) of the western part of the country. The design of our study was based on three groups of independent variables: (1) socio-structural, with questions on occupation, income etc.; (2) socio-cultural, with questions on education, religious affiliation, etc. and (3) psychological, with questions determining rigidity, severity, etc.

The dependent variables comprised for the Belgian study 42 and for the Dutch sample 52 questions pertaining to attitudes toward rules of law; these questions are listed on pages 23 to 27. In this we partially followed the study by Podgorecki, in which questions were asked regarding rules of law in the fields of moral judgement (e.g. euthanasia, abortion), socio-economics, and social engineering. The contrast between these fields of legislation is highly relevant to our hypotheses. While the former is traditional and a part of the culture in question, the other two arose mainly from industrialization, and their orientation is therefore instrumental in nature.

It is consistent with our hypotheses that the attitudes towards the traditional type of legislation are less heterogeneous and less differentiated than those adopted towards the mainly collective type generated by industrialization.

To the questions which we borrowed from Podgorecki, we added a number of others concerning fiscal laws. This increased the comparability with an earlier study performed in Leiden.[30]

The respondents were asked to give their opinion of a number

19

of acts constituting violations of the law. A respondent could express his disapproval and estimation of punishment according to the five-part response of the Likert scale.

For the analysis of the material we did not apply an *a priori* classification, but one based on a factor analysis of the responses and giving a greater coherence between the questions. We shall return to this point later.

DIVERGENT ATTITUDES REGARDING A NUMBER OF RULES OF LAW

Comparison of the results of the Belgian and Dutch studies

The general results of the Belgian and Dutch studies will be discussed in this section. For the widest possible comparison of the two sets of results, we applied a rank order. The Spearman-rank correlation coefficient gave a value of $r=0.926$ for 'disapproval' [D.APP] and of $r=0.876$ for 'punishment advocated' [PUN].

Classification of the offences according to the degree of a tendency towards disapproval and towards advocacy of punishment. The offences were classified according to the tendency to advocate punishment, because punishment lies closer to the sphere of law and disapproval more in the moral sphere. According to the results, these tendencies vary widely from offence to offence. For 70% of the Belgian respondents, 12 offences were held to require punishment, and for 90% at least two of them were. In the Netherlands, 14 offences were considered punishable by 70%, and two of them by more than 90% of the respondents. Whereas 50–69% of the Belgian respondents deemed 10 offences worthy of punishment, a similar proportion of the Dutch sample extended this opinion to 14 offences. Again, of the Belgian respondents 30–49% found 16 offences punishable as against 10 for a commensurate percentage of the Dutch respondents. Four offences were considered punishable by less than 29% of the Belgian respondents, the response being the same in the Netherlands.

Thus, the Belgian population showed less tendency to advocate punishment, a finding which may be partially explained by the fact
20

that the Belgian sample, unlike the Dutch sample, did not include any woman or residents of rural areas.

These general results suggest that empirically, a general 'sense of justice' does not exist. The reaction to the various legal rules differed widely, in some cases there was even no majority opinion. This multiformity and multidimensionality of the sense of justice was made an integral part of our study.

Relationship between disapproval and tendency to advocate sanctions. Through this relationship, the relationship between moral values[31] and a sense of justice can be approached. The term moral is used in its widest sense. Below, we will use it in a stricter sense. It is generally assumed that advocacy of punishment is stricter than disapproval. It is only with respect to certain offences against moral values that the sanctioning apparatus of penal law is supposed to react. A sense of justice is usually considered to imply consciousness of moral values. Punishment generally assumes disapproval. The reverse does not hold, however, as is clearly shown by the results of the studies in Belgium and the Netherlands. The percentage of respondents disapproving of an offence is always higher than the percentage advocating punishment for that offence, although of course, this does not necessarily mean that each individual respondent disapproves more frequently than he advocates punishment. In the Dutch study we found that on correlating each question concerning disapproval and punishment, a small percentage of respondents (varying from 0·3 for perjury to 6·7 for smuggling of cigarettes) did not disapprove of the offence but nevertheless thought it deserved punishment. This type of attitude we call the legalistic acceptance of rules of law: the offence is not rejected morally, but punishment is considered to be required, probably because it is thought that too many of such offences (e.g. smuggling, poaching) would dislocate society. In addition to this type, we distinguished complete acceptance (both disapproval and advocacy of punishment), limited acceptance (disapproval without punishment), and complete rejection (no disapproval and no punishment). In the full report on the study done in the Netherlands this point will be discussed in detail. Here, it will suffice to remark that our results do indicate that the acceptance of law is by no means uniform; only 30 of the 52 legal rules included in the investigation were completely accepted by 50% or more of the respondents. The

21

more general the moral values, the more necessary sanctions seem to be. The more often a given offence is disapproved of, the more often it is judged to be punishable. The results show unequivocally that this hypothesis is confirmed by our study. The percentage of respondents disapproving of certain behaviour is proportional to the percentage demanding application of sanctions. The rank correlation is unusually high: $r=0.925$ for Belgium and $r=0.876$ for the Netherlands.

The intensity of disapproval and advocacy of sanctions. It is evident from the foregoing that a multiple legal and moral consciousness exists. This raises the question of the extremes of this consciousness. This problem can be approached by analysis of the percentage of respondents whose answers rated the higher score (code 5: 'I disapprove very strongly, I would punish very heavily'). This is the percentage of individuals who disapprove of the offence very strongly and think it should be punished very severely. Most of the Belgian and Dutch respondents chose score 4, the less extreme answer; they disapproved of the offence less strongly and thought it deserved less severe punishment. With few exceptions, the percentage of extreme scores (5) is lower than the less extreme score (4) and indeed, the former does not even total 25%. Thus, in questions of law and morals Belgian and Dutch people do not seem to be extremists.

Opinion on punishment and disapproval with respect to various offences

Offences considered deserving of punishment by 70–100% of the Belgian respondents (Table 1A). As indicated by Table 1A, in this first group we find mainly offences involving danger to human life (failure to give aid in possibly fatal situations, violation of safety rules, driving under the influence of alcohol), but also deliberate falsification and refusal to co-operate with the legal system. The last of these evoked strong disapproval and was considered to deserve severe punishment in both countries, there being in general little difference between disapproval and punishment. This strictness may be surprising. It fails to confirm the assumption that
22

citizens are not willingly inclined to help support the system.

Violation of safety rules was considered punishable by more than 75% of the respondents in both countries, and disapproval was very strong. This reaction is possibly explained by the fact that such violations endanger the physical safety of the workers.

TABLE 1A: *Disapproval and the tendency to advocate Punishment: Offences considered Deserving of Punishment by 70–100% of Belgian respondents.*[1]

	Dutch Sample		Belgian Sample	
Items[2]	Dis-approval %	Punish-ment %	Dis-approval %	Punish-ment %
Someone drives a car after his driver's licence has been taken away.	96·3	92·8	96·73	94·33
Someone commits perjury.	98·0	96·0	95·00	92·38
Someone fails to help another person who is in mortal danger although he could do so.	98·6	76·2	96·95	86·52
Someone drives his car without having paid the road-tax.	89·7	80·0	88·47	81·08
A driver exceeds the speed-limit within the city limits.	91·7	86·3	86·29	79·56
Someone fakes his accounts by shifting a decimal point. The income figure for his tax-return is reduced by 10·000 guilders as a result of this manipulation.	94·4	88·5	80·65	76·73
Someone disregards the safety regulations in a factory.	98·4	81·5	94·77	76·51
Someone disregards the pedestrian traffic light.	95·0	81·1	89·34	75·86
Someone takes drugs.	89·0	74·0	84·56	75·86
Someone does not tell the police the name of a criminal.	92·8	79·7	86·73	75·43
Someone fails to appear before the court in order to give evidence, without duly informing the court.	85·4	53·6	85·86	74·77
Someone drives his car after drinking six glasses of beer.	93·7	88·9	73·90	70·86

[1] In this and in the following tables, findings are presented in order of decreasing percentages in the Belgian survey. For the reader's convenience this bulky material has also been broken up into separate tables based on percentage interval scales applicable to the Belgian study.

[2] Where necessary, items are adjusted to take account of the local situation in Belgium and the Netherlands.

23

In this group typical differences between the Netherlands and Belgium were found with respect to driving under the influence of alcohol (much more strongly disapproved of in the Netherlands by 74–94%, and more often considered punishable there than in Belgium, i.e. by 71–89%; unwillingness to give evidence in court was, however, considered punishable more often in Belgium, i.e. by 75% as against 54% in the Netherlands.

The group of offences considered punishable by 50–70% of the Belgian respondents (Table 1B). This group comprises a number of

TABLE 1B: *Disapproval and the tendency to advocate Punishment: Offences considered Deserving of Punishment by 50–70% of Belgian respondents.*

	Dutch Sample		Belgian Sample	
Items	Dis- approval %	Punish- ment %	Dis- approval %	Punish- ment %
Someone changes a receipt for 10 guilders into 100 guilders in order to deduct this amount from his taxable income.	93·5	75·2	79·70	68·66
Someone receives sickness benefits for a full week due to an administrative error, although he has already returned to work. He does not send the money back.	92·7	68·8	81·29	65·64
Someone sells liquor without the requisite permit.	82·0	74·5	68·91	62·51
Someone has not registered his radio and TV sets.	82·3	64·3	69·12	56·94
Someone does not allow the revenue office to investigate his accounts.	87·5	59·0	71·08	54·99
Someone back-dates a receipt for tax deduction purposes.	76·0	57·1	65·65	53·69
A soldier is absent without leave for two days.	70·2	54·1	61·73	52·81
Someone keeps his 13-year-old daughter at home to do housework, although she is still of school age.	85·7	51·4	74·99	51·08
Someone orders his workmen to work overtime without a permit.	49·1	37·8	60·64	50·86
Someone smuggles 10 cartons of cigarettes (purchased tax-free) through the customs.	67·7	61·2	54·99	50·64

fiscal offences and two socio-economic offences (overtime work without official permission and taking unentitled sick-pay), one offence having to do with the licensing system, and evasion of compulsory military service and of school attendance.

A two-thirds majority considered that anyone receiving a week's sick-pay due to an administrative error even though he had already returned to work, should be penalized. A very high percentage expressed disapproval of such behaviour. The smuggling of ten cartons of cigarettes was considered punishable by a small majority in Belgium and by a larger majority in the Netherlands.

In contrast with the Netherlands, a majority in Belgium thought that an employer who required his employees to work overtime illegally should be punished.

Otherwise, there were no marked differences between the percentages in the two countries.

Group of offences considered punishable by 30–50% of the Belgian respondents (Table 1C). The chief offences in this group are illegal abortion, adultery, and euthanasia, which will be discussed separately later. The other offences included several fiscal items. Stiffer punishments were advocated for physicians in Belgium than in the Netherlands (48% as against 33%), failure to report large extra earnings was disapproved of more strongly in the Netherlands (51% as against 68%), and in the Netherlands paying cash with a discount for automobile repairs was regarded with more disapproval and assigned a heavier punishment (49% and 73% to 38% and 59% respectively).

Among the violations, keeping a pub open after hours received less disapproval in Belgium (53% as against 72%) and this also held for punishment. For poaching, the differences in the percentages for the two countries were very large: in Belgium only 45% advocated punishment as against 71% in the Netherlands. But the reverse was the case for the violations of building codes (35% in Belgium as against 20% in the Netherlands).

Group of offences considered punishable by less than 30% of the Belgian respondents (Table 1D). This group of offences includes fishing without a licence, reporting sick without cause, and two tax offences involving failure to report small extra earnings. Strong disapproval was expressed in the Netherlands about reporting sick

25

TABLE 1C: *Disapproval and the tendency to advocate Punishment: Offences considered Deserving of Punishment by 30–50% of Belgian respondents.*

Items	Dutch Sample		Belgian Sample	
	Dis-approval %	Punish-ment %	Dis-approval %	Punish-ment %
A doctor performs an abortion.	68·4	61·9	52·60	49·12
A doctor redecorates his office and his living-room. All costs are booked as expenditure for his practice.	56·0	33·0	64·56	48·47
Someone fails to report for his first military service without giving reason.	78·4	55·2	69·12	47·38
Someone commits adultery.	81·8	53·3	64·77	46·30
Someone earns 5000 guilders a year extra by working overtime, but does not report this on his tax return.	68·0	57·8	50·64	45·43
Someone poaches.	75·4	71·3	51·51	44·77
Someone keeps his pub open after closing time.	72·0	55·3	53·26	43·04
Someone picks flowers from a municipal park.	72·0	43·5	60·21	41·08
Someone visited a relative in a place where he had a short business talk. He stayed at a hotel and dined out with his relation several times. The expenditure for all this was about 350 guilders. He records this amount as business expenditure.	71·6	45·7	60·21	40·86
Someone violates price regulations by selling below the minimum price.	48·5	38·0	48·04	38·90
Someone repairs cars for cash. He asks his clients whether they want a receipt. If not, he deducts a small amount from the bill and also from the figures he books as income.	73·2	59·0	49·34	38·25
Someone unexpectedly exceeds the 'wage-limit'. He does not reveal the increase in his income when he files his tax return.	61·9	42·2	48·90	37·60
Someone disregards the municipal building regulations by making a sky-light without a permit.	35·7	20·1	41·94	35·43
Someone disregards the 'no entrance' notice on the grounds of an estate.	52·4	29·8	48·92	32·82
Someone allows an incurable patient to die at the patient's request.	50·9	32·2	42·17	32·38
Someone joins a demonstration for which no permit has been obtained.	61·2	35·3	46·30	31·08

26

without cause (75% as against 49% in Belgium), and the same was the case for failure to report extra earnings.

TABLE 1D : *Disapproval and the tendency to advocate Punishment: Offences considered Deserving of Punishment by less than 30% of Belgian respondents.*

Items	Dutch Sample		Belgian Sample	
	Dis-approval %	Punish-ment %	Dis-approval %	Punish-ment %
Someone fishes without a fishing licence.	34·7	23·1	34·77	28·47
Someone reports himself ill with a slight cold, but in fact he wants a day's rest.	75·2	37·6	49·34	25·86
Someone earns 1000 guilders by doing extra work. He does not report this amount on his tax return.	51·4	38·5	33·69	25·86
A wage-earner does odd jobs on his own account in his spare time, earning 500 guilders a year extra. He does not record this income on his tax return.	30·0	19·3	21·51	14·77

Violation of laws pertaining to morals. It we consider laws pertaining to morals as well as the above-mentioned and the use of drugs, we see a class of law lying in the domain of what we would call moral judgements: all of them concern life and sexuality. They all belong to a domain traditionally perceived as pre-eminently moral in a stricter sense. Violation of these laws would offend what Durkheim calls the *conscience collective*. Whether this 'traditional morality' actually permeated the lives and ideas of people in times past is of course impossible to say on the basis of the present study. What we can determine is current ideas about violations of moral laws which, it is said, are at present in the process of being re-evaluated.

The degree of disapproval and of advocacy of punishment can be measured on the basis of four categories: a two-thirds majority, an absolute majority, a relative majority or no majority at all. By two-thirds we mean the cases in which the percentage advocating punishment or disapproving is higher than 66·6%. By absolute majority we mean a percentage higher than 50% but less than 66·6%. By relative majority we mean the cases in which the percentage advocating punishment or disapproving is higher than the percentage not advocating punishment or disapproving but is less than 50%. Finally we have the cases in which there are none of the above mentioned majorities.

TABLE 2: *Differences between the Netherlands and Belgium in disapproval and advocacy of punishment with respect to rules of law in the field of moral judgement.*

	Belgium		The Netherlands	
Offence	Punishment advocated	Disapproval	Punishment advocated	Disapproval
Aid in the presence of danger	$\frac{2}{3}$ majority	$\frac{2}{3}$ majority	$\frac{2}{3}$ majority	$\frac{2}{3}$ majority
Drugs	$\frac{2}{3}$ majority	$\frac{2}{3}$ majority	$\frac{2}{3}$ majority	$\frac{2}{3}$ majority
Abortion	rel. majority	abs. majority	abs. majority	$\frac{2}{3}$ majority
Adultery	rel. majority	abs. majority	abs. majority	$\frac{2}{3}$ majority
Euthanasia	no majority	rel. majority	no majority	abs. majority

In both countries a two-thirds majority thought that refusal to give aid in the presence of mortal danger, and the use of drugs, deserved disapproval and punishment. There was wide consensus on this point, but less with respect to abortion and adultery, which an absolute majority disapproved of in Belgium but only a relative majority considered should be penalized by the courts. In the Netherlands a two-thirds majority disapproved of both, but only an absolute majority advocated punishment. Two explanations, not necessarily contradictory, can be offered for this phenomenon: changing patterns of morality and/or sense of justice. Here it is assumed that new ideas will in time replace the old standards, but in the meantime a pluralism develops in which two or more concepts are opposed, i.e. newer against older. Such an interpretation is supported by the fact that opinions for and against moral laws concerning life and sexuality are very strong.

Lastly, neither Belgium nor the Netherlands had even a relative majority advocating punishment for acceding to an incurably sick patient's request to be allowed to die. Disapproval was shown by a relative majority in Belgium and by a barely absolute majority in the Netherlands.

Fiscal offences. Like the preceding class of laws, fiscal laws require separate consideration, in our opinion. We find them at both the top and the bottom of the list of offences arranged according to the degree of punishment. The rank correlation between the Belgian and Dutch results is high (D.APP: r=0·88; PUN: r=0·89). This wide range with respect to the degree of advocacy of punishment for, and disapproval of, fiscal offences offers us an approach to the problem of the relationship between opinion and behaviour. To keep up appearances, disapproval of certain fiscal offences is expressed, but when it comes to deeds the same individual has no scruple about committing them.

The results indicate that the various offences are disapproved of to varying degrees and are considered to deserve varying degrees of punishment. Experience has shown that certain types of offences are committed more often than others. If it were to be found that the most frequent fiscal offences receive the least disapproval and advocacy of punishment, if conversely, the least frequent fiscal offences receive the most disapproval and advocacy of punishment, then it could be said that there was a relationship between opinion and behaviour with respect to fiscal matters.

What we actually know is the following:

(1) Failure to report extra earning is universal and receives little disapproval or recommendation of punishment.
(2) Manipulations (i.e. misleading calculation of costs) probably occur frequently. A majority disapprove but do not consider them punishable.
(3) Deliberate falsification occurs but is usually avoided. This offence is disapproved of and considered punishable by a (large) majority.

Thus, there seems to be a correlation between behaviour and opinion. This is not of course meant to imply that some of those who consider an offence to be punishable would not commit it themselves.

Comparison with several legal criteria

Legal sanctions versus disapproval and advocacy of punishment. Comparison of these two factors makes it possible to determine whether the law penalizes an act more severely the more widespread is the opinion that the offence is serious. At the same time, it is possible to detect a possible discrepancy between the external definition of the criminal character of an act and the subjective definition applied to it by the majority.

We may assume that the more severe the maximum penalty set by law, the more strongly the offence is disapproved of and the more strongly punishment is advocated.

In the Netherlands the degree to which a given law is accepted is dependent on the penalty prescribed for the offence by law. But despite the general tendency, rather wide differences are found for individual crimes.

The Belgian results too show clearly that the discrepancy between legislation and public opinion is not as great as is often thought. The advocacy of (corrective) punishment for misdemeanours is distinctly greater than that for petty offences. Among misdemeanours those carrying a prison sentence are more generally considered worthy of punishment than those calling for a fine.

The amount of time which has elapsed since passage of a law. In the Netherlands the hypothesis holds to some extent that the longer a given law has been in effect, the greater the acceptance of that law. The character of the law probably plays a large part in this. Of the myriad existing laws, many such as forgery, refusal of aid in mortal danger, and failure to give evidence have a moral basis. But many of the laws passed since the Second World War concern socio-economic and socio-technical regulations arising less directly from moral judgements. Violations of these laws receive much less disapproval. The hypothesis is not however valid for Belgium. There, the character of the law is of decisive importance.

ATTITUDES TOWARDS RULES OF LAW WITHIN SOCIAL GROUPS

Classification of the data according to type of offence

Earlier we have seen that the attitude towards rules of law is dependent on the character of these rules. We came to this conclusion on the basis of a comparison of the disapproval and advocacy of punishment for each of certain rules of law individually. If we extend this analysis by adding the independent variables of income, occupation, education, age, rigidity and severity of personality, separate consideration of the laws in question gives a confusing if comprehensive picture since details carry too much weight. To obtain a more generalized picture, we attempted to find a common denominator for the dependent variables (i.e. the 42 questions in the Belgian study and the 52 in the Dutch study), by forming groups of rules of law of the same sociological and legal nature. Therefore the data as a whole were subsequently subjected to a factor analysis so that the questions could be grouped according to types within which they had a certain degree of correlation.

In the Dutch study the following types of rules emerged: rules concerning neglect of important duties, rules falling in the field of moral judgement, fiscal rules, the so-called minor offences, and a few rules concerning traffic and alcohol. In the Belgian study the same type of rules resulted from the factor analysis except rules which concern neglect of important duties. The dependent variables (i.e. the answers to the questions concerning disapproval and advocacy of punishment) within the types were combined using Likert's method, the score for each type indicating the degree of disapproval of violation of the given rules. We also calculated a score for the advocacy of punishment.

Comparison of the acceptance of various types of rules of law in Belgium and the Netherlands

Rules concerning neglect of important duties. In specifying the attitude towards various types of rules of law characterized by the factor analysis, we give precedence to the rules concerning neglect

31

of important duties. This type (e.g. summons to appear in court, safety measures protecting employees, compulsory education) belongs to a category having great importance in our legal culture. Consequently, it offers an initial point of orientation for our total view of the attitude of various groups concerning rules of many different kinds.

Table 3 gives a condensed picture on the basis of three groups of scores. We indicated three degrees of disapproval, and did the same in case of the advocacy of punishment. In the Belgian survey, which had fewer interviewees than the Dutch study, the type of law concerning neglect of important duties was not as clearly expressed in the factor analysis as in the Dutch survey.

TABLE 3: *Comparison of the degree of disapproval and advocacy of punishment in relation to rules concerning neglect of important duties in Belgium and in the Netherlands.*

Attitude	Disapproval		Advocacy of punishment	
	Belgium %	The Netherlands %	Belgium %	The Netherlands %
Weak	—	—	—	2·1
Moderate	4·5	6·4	12·2	39·6
Strong	95·5	93·6	87·8	58·3
Total percentage	100·0	100·0	100·0	100·0
n*	197	644	197	644

Chi Square disapproval $= 0.94$ df $= 2$ $0.50 > p > 0.30$ (not significant)
Chi Square punishment $= 4.26$ df $= 2$ $0.05 > p > 0.02$ (significant)
* For sake of comparability, the percentages concern only men. In the Dutch survey, however, both women and men were interviewed.

The results indicate that there is a highly postive attitude towards this type of law in the population. This is even more striking if it is kept in mind that in this context the respondents were not expressing opinions about serious crimes, involving laws which assume a homogeneous orientation with respect to cultural values. It is also noteworthy that strong disapproval was expressed much more often than punishment was advocated.

Table 4 shows the same consensus with respect to these laws as

TABLE 4: *Relationship between some independent variables and the attitude towards rules of law concerning neglect of important duties in the Netherlands.*

	Disapproval	Advocacy of punishment
Income	not significant	not significant
Occupation	idem	idem
Education	idem	idem
Age	idem	$>$ age $<$ punishment
Rigidity[32]	idem	not significant
Severity[32]	idem	$>$ severity $>$ punishment

is found in Table 3. None of the independent variables exerts an influence on the degree of disapproval, and only two variables are divergent. The older the individual, the less severe the punishment considered proper r=−0·05); there is a positive correlation between the degree of severity and advocacy of punishment (r=0·10).

Rules in the field of moral judgement. In addition to the type of law relating to rules concerning neglect of important duties, the factor analysis showed a category lying in the field of moral judgement, e.g. euthanasia, performance of abortion, adultery, use of drugs. In Belgium the use of drugs was omitted from the scale construction. We may perhaps say that the rules concerning neglect of important duties are generally based in society itself, whereas rules in the field of moral judgement are more closely connected with the doctrines of the church and with moral theology. If these are secularized and lose their authority the question arises of the extent to which theologically oriented rules will become the subject of open discussion.

Table 5 does not reflect any general acceptance, since disapproval of offences against rules concerning moral judgement were disapproved of by only a third of the Belgian respondents, and about half of the Dutch respondents. Not quite a third advocated severe penalties. The high intermediate percentages are striking, the more so when Tables 3 and 5 are compared. The male Dutch respondents were significantly more disapproving and more severe in penalizing than the Belgian respondents. This is perhaps related to the fact that rural respondents were included in the Netherlands, whereas the Belgian survey was confined to Antwerp and its

33

TABLE 5: *Comparison of the degree of disapproval and advocacy of punishment with respect to the rules in the field of moral judgement in Belgium and the Netherlands.*

Attitude	Disapproval		Advocacy of punishment	
	Belgium %	The Netherlands %	Belgium %	The Netherlands %
Weak	12·1	5·6	20·8	12·5
Moderate	50·4	42·4	51·3	55·5
Strong	37·5	52·0	27·9	32·0
Total percentage	100·0	100·0	100·0	100·0
n	197	644	197	644

Chi square disapproval = 17·8   df = 2 $p < 0.001$ (significant)
Chi square punishment = 8·7   df = 2 $0.01 < p < 0.02$ (significant)

environs. The Dutch study also shows that women were significantly more disapproving than men but not more severe with respect to punishment.

In the Belgian survey, moral judgement was only significant as a dimension with respect to advocacy of punishment. Here, a significant correlation coefficient was found for only three variables, namely (in order of magnitude of the correlation) rigidity, religious affiliation and severity. On the basis of this significance the fol-

TABLE 6: *Relationship between some independent variables and attitude towards laws in the field of moral judgement in the Netherlands.* *

	Disapproval		Advocacy of punishment	
Income	> income	< disapproval	> income	< punishment
Occupation	> occupation	< disapproval	> occupation	< punishment
Education	> education	< disapproval	> education	< punishment
Age	> age	> disapproval	not significant	
Rigidity	> rigidity	> disapproval	> rigidity	> punishment
Severity	> severity	> disapproval	> severity	> punishment

*For statistical reasons, in the Belgian survey, a random sample was taken from the original stratified sample. As a result, certain categories based on the scales of the variables mentioned (age, occupation, income, etc.) were too small to permit determination of statistical significance. Thus, Tables 6, 8 and 10 concern only the Dutch respondents. For the rest of the tables the original sample was used.

lowing conclusions may be drawn. The degree of Catholicity is positively correlated with the degree of advocacy of punishment in the field of moral judgement. If we distinguish between practising Catholic, non-practising Catholic, and non-Catholic, we see a descending order of advocacy of punishment with respect to this type of law. Secondly, rigidity and severity are both positively correlated with advocacy of punishment in this context. The more rigid or severe an individual, the stronger the advocacy of punishment. It should also be mentioned that there is only a very low correlation between severity and rigidity themselves.

With respect to the Dutch results, it may be mentioned that 25·1% of the respondents who said they never went to church and 67·5% of those who went to church six or more times a month, strongly disapproved of the offences in question. For severe punishment, these figures were 45·5% and 79·7%, respectively. On the basis of the social variables, the Netherlands shows significant differences in attitude. Table 6 shows that the middle and higher occupational groups are more moderate in their reactions than the other groups, including small shopkeepers. In our opinion, this constitutes confirmation of Ranulf's theory[31] that social insecurity of lower middle-class groups is correlated with greater advocacy of punishment. The figures also point in the direction of a positive correlation between educational level and tolerance with respect to unspecified moral offences. As Table 6 indicates, age is positively correlated with disapproval, but any correlation with punishment is not significant.

Fiscal rules. Great diversity was also found in connection with another area, namely, fiscal laws. It would be difficult to find anyone who was not convinced that some kind of taxation is necessary. Taxes form the 'life blood'[33] of government. Nevertheless, there is a certain fear of strong tax administration and the taxpayer is thought to require protection in this respect. Here the analogy with penal law is inescapable. Both are construed as restrictive. In both, the state is in opposition to the individual, and in an ambivalent way. Although the justification for penal law lies in the protection which it affords to person and goods, it is not inconceivable that the price demanded by the State for serving the individual is too high.[33] Taxation is a condition for good government, the more so because of the great number of functions involved and the decisive importance of the national budget in a welfare state. But it seems possible that the heavy financial burden the State places on the individual leaves him too little freedom.

Against this background of the ambivalent character of fiscal laws, we included in our survey a number of questions concerning tax evasion in the form of failure to report sources of income and incorrect reporting of income (e.g. falsification of bills).

TABLE 7: *Comparison of the degree of disapproval and advocacy of punishment with respect to fiscal rules in Belgium and in the Netherlands.*

Attitude	Disapproval		Advocacy of punishment	
	Belgium	The Netherlands	Belgium	The Netherlands
Weak	7·1	2·6	12·7	7·0
Moderate	62·5	38·3	68·5	57·8
Strong	30·4	59·1	18·8	35·2
Total percentage	100·0	100·0	100·0	100·0
n	197	644	197	644

Chi square disapproval $= 54·24$ $df = 2$ $p < 0·001$ (significant)
Chi square punishment $= 21·11$ $df = 2$ $p < 0·001$ (significant)

Comparison of the percentages in Table 7 with those in Table 3 shows that acceptance of fiscal law is only moderate. Comparison with Table 5 shows that a lower percentage of the Belgian respondents strongly disapprove of violation of fiscal laws or advocate severe punishment than in the field of moral judgement. Conversely, the Dutch males show greater fidelity to fiscal than to moral rules,

TABLE 8: *Relationship between some independent variables and attitude towards fiscal rules in the Netherlands.*

	Disapproval		Advocacy of punishment	
Income	> income	< disapproval	> income	< punishment
Occupation	> occupation	> disapproval	> occupation	> punishment
Education	> education	> disapproval	> education	> punishment
Age	> age	> disapproval	> age	> punishment
Rigidity	> rigidity	> disapproval	> rigidity	> punishment
Severity	> severity	> disapproval	not significant	

i.e. significantly more of them disapprove of and consider offences of this kind punishable than do the Belgian males.

Although the Belgian figures are not mentioned in Table 8, the difference in attitude between the Dutch and Belgian respondents indicated in Table 7 is also present in this section. Reservation concerning fiscal rules in Belgium occurs similarly in various groups; only a few independent variables show a significant difference in attitude. In the Netherlands, to the contrary, significant differences were found in virtually all respects.

It may also be mentioned that in both countries entrepreneurs and members of the upper middle-class are less disapproving of fiscal offences than wage-earners. In Belgium, respondents with large incomes were more disapproving and advocated more severe punishment more often than the lower income groups.

For the Dutch survey, the correlation between the figures for the various income groups and those for the degree of disapproval is not linear. Both the highest and the lowest income groups showed 60–65% strong disapproval of fiscal violations, whereas for the other groups the percentage lay between 49% and 56%.

The higher level population group (with respect to occupation, and education) had a more positive attitude towards fiscal rules than the other groups. Several suggestions can be made about this point. The former group may have a better understanding of taxation[35] and governmental expenditure while the lower level groups may exaggerate tax pressures. The latter is suggested by the results of an earlier study done in the Netherlands.[36] Another supposition is that the greater possibilities for legal forms of evasion at the disposal of the higher status group[37] leads the lower status groups to emphasize the apparent aspects of the social elements in modern taxation. Verification of these assumptions requires further research.

Petty offences. The fourth category of law to emerge from the factor analysis is much less homogeneous than the two we have just discussed. It includes trespassing, failure of military personnel to report for duty on time, fishing without a licence and the like. Violations of these rules may be called petty offences, but they are nevertheless of interest in the present context. They are needed to control social behaviour in a wider sense. They are indispensable in that with populations of the size confronting us at present, they provide a minimum of balance both between one man's freedom to enjoy his property and the vexatious consequences of his enjoyment for another man, and between freedom of consumption and conspicuous consumption. In this respect too, the free play of forces cannot be reconciled with an industrialized society; in this kind of society a series of trivial rules must be respected. But a tangled web of such rules, made worse by a plethora of petty officials, creates the danger of an inflation of rules, which will ultimately undermine the integrity of more important laws.

TABLE 9: *Comparison of the degree of disapproval and advocacy of punishment with respect to petty offences in Belgium and the Netherlands.*

Attitude	Disapproval		Advocacy of punishment	
	Belgium	The Netherlands	Belgium	The Netherlands
Weak	14·2	17·4	21·3	36·5
Moderate	65·0	68·4	65·4	57·4
Strong	20·8	14·2	13·3	6·1
Total percentage	100·0	100·0	100·0	100·0
n	197	644	197	644

Chi square disapproval = 5·45 df = 2 $0·10 > p > 0·05$ (not significant)
Chi square punishment = 22·74 df = 2 $p < 0·001$ (significant)

Only a small number of both the Dutch and the Belgian respondents disapproved strongly of such offences, and even fewer thought they should be punished severely. But in both countries the score for mild punishment shows a higher percentage than that for mild disapproval. Nonetheless, the figures in Table 9 do not

TABLE 10: *Relationship between some independent variables and the attitude toward petty offences in the Netherlands.*

	Disapproval		Advocacy of punishment	
Income	> income	< disapproval	> income	< punishment
Occupation	> occupation	< disapproval	not significant	
Education	> education	< disapproval	idem	
Age	> age	> disapproval	idem	
Rigidity	> rigidity	> disapproval	> rigidity	> punishment
Severity	> severity	> disapproval	> severity	> punishment

point to a legalistic attitude; there is a small degree of inner acceptance of this type of law.

It is also clear from Table 9 that there is no significant difference in the disapproval of the Dutch and Belgian males, but the Belgian respondents were significantly more severe in the amount of punishment they advocated.

The higher income, educational, and occupational groups had a more negative attitude towards petty offences than the opposite groups: the most powerful factor being the income of the respondents. The higher income groups are less disapproving and prescribe less severe punishment than the other groups (r disapp.= – 0·05; r pun. = – 0·06, for the Dutch survey). The independent variable of age and the psychological variables exert a positive influence on the degree of acceptance of this type of rule. The relationships we found were roughly the same for the two countries. In Belgium the attitude towards petty offences is highly dependent on the respondent's age: the older the individual, the stronger the disapproval and the more severe the punishment recommended. Here, the psychological variables also have a positive influence: the more rigid and strict respondents disapprove more strongly and think such offences deserve more severe penalties. Income, in contrast, works in the other direction: the higher the income the less the acceptance of this type of rule.

CONCLUSIONS

The very character of theories of law makes it to some extent inevitable that the legitimization of rules of law is regarded holistically. Many scholars of law and sociology who discuss the acceptance of rules of law, maintain such concepts as 'moral judgement', 'social pressure', and 'law' as a totality. The present results make it more than clear that the attitudes towards various types of rules of law diverge widely. The hypotheses on which the survey was based are verified. Only the rules pertaining to neglect of important duties were universally accepted. Rules in the field of moral judgement, however much rooted in tradition, no longer enjoy general social adhesion; we might even say that a large part of the population sees this type of 'victimless'[38] offence as only partially a matter of government authority. This is perhaps a sign of a cultural shift in the direction of greater freedom or of a more pluralistic culture.[39]

On the basis of the results of the factor analysis, fiscal rules may be considered as a separate category of legal rule, but there is wide divergence in the disapproval of and punishment prescribed for individual offences. Thus, for instance, fiscal fraud is not regarded homogeneously. Failure to report income receives little disapproval and is not considered highly punishable, but deliberate falsification is disapproved of and considered to deserve punishment by a large majority. The former probably commonly occurs, the latter is preferably avoided. This too illustrates the correlation between behaviour and opinion. The divergence with respect to falsification, failure to report income and the like, points to a belief in due process on a high level regardless of whether tax administrators are concerned. But it also conveys the existence of a desire for a margin of individual financial freedom, an area in which taxation policies do not intrude.

The attitudes found with respect to petty offences provide grounds for an analogous assumption. Further research on attitudes towards 'collective laws' is required, not least of all because it may be expected that these laws will eventually take on international dimensions. In this connection it should be kept in mind that our cross-national study has shown that there is a high degree of divergence with respect to disapproval and punishment regarding fiscal laws even in two countries as closely related as Belgium and the Netherlands.

We consider research on the acceptance of rules of law, and in particular on attitudes towards laws characteristic of our welfare state, to be the first order of business in the field of the sociology law. Another subject requiring study is that of social behaviour in the context of law. In the future, special attention will also have to be given to the legal system, not least of all to legal organizations, including the administrative executive organs of both business and government.

NOTES

1. E. M. Schur, *Law and Society*, New York; Random House (1969) pp. 177–182.
   R. Treves and J. F. Glastra van Loon, *Norms and Actions*, Den Haag; Nijhoff (1968).
2. A. Podgorecki, The Prestige of the Law, (Preliminary Research Results) *Acta Sociologica*, Copenhagen; Munksgaard (1967) vol. 10 fasc. 1–2 p. 81.
3. W. Friedman, *Legal Theory*, London; Stevens and Sons (1967) pp. 29 and 85.
4. G. E. Langiemeijer, *Inleiding tot de studie van de wijsbegeerte des Rechts*, Zwolle; Tjeenk Willink (1970) pp. 149 and 150.
5. H. Krabbe, *Het Rechtsgezag*, Den Haag (1917) p. 53.
6. L. L. Fuller, *The Morality of the Law*, New Haven; Yale University Press (1963) p. 162.
7. Ph. Selznick, *Law, Society and Industrial Justice*, New York; Russell Sage Foundation (1969) p. 17.
8. H. L. A. Hart, *The Concept of Law*, Oxford; Oxford University Press (1961) p. 84.
9. A. V. Dicey, *Law and public opinion in England*, London; Macmillan (1963) pp. 21, 22, 41.
10. H. V. Ball, C. E. Simpson, K. Ikeda, Law and Social change: Sumner Reconsidered, *American Journal of Sociology*, Chicago; University of Chicago Press, 1961–2 vol. 67 p. 538.
11. H. Kelsen, *Reine Rechtslehre*, Vienna; Deuticke (1967) p. 111.
12. H. Hernes, Die Funktion des Rechts in der modernen Gesellschaft, *Acta Sociologica*, Copenhagen; Munksgaard (1971) vol. 14 no. 4 p. 274.
13. R. Rolland, *Jean Christophe*, Paris; Ed. Albin Michel, (1931) tome 2, p. 405.
14. C. Wright Mills, *The Sociological Imagination*, London; Penguin Books (1959) pp. 12 and 13.
15. J. B. Grossman, M. Grossman, *Law and Change in Modern America*, California; Goodyear Publishing Company Inc., (1971) p. 4.
16. Talcott Parsons, The Law and Social Control, W. M. Evan ed. *Law and Sociology*, New York; The Free Press of Glencoe (1962) p. 62.
17. G. E. Langemeijer, Wat kan de rechtsfilosofie nu nog presteren?, *Wending*, Den Haag; January (1972).
18. J. Van Houtte, De rechtssociologie, haar ambities en beperkingen, *Tijdschrift voor Privaatrecht*, Gent (1970) no. 4, p. 419.
19. A. Shonfield, *Modern Capitalism*, Oxford; Oxford University Press (1965) p. 67.
20. *Wenkend Perspectief*, Ned. Verbond van vakverenigingen, Amsterdam (1957) p. 369.
21. ibid. A. Shonfield, no. 19 p. 6.
22. P. Vinke, Impressions from Abroad, *Journal of Legal Education*, Lexington (1971) vol. 23 p. 211.
23. F. Van Heek, *Inleidingscollege Macrosociologie*, Sociologisch Instituut Leiden (1969).
    E. K. Francis, *Wissenschaftliche Grundlagen Soziologischen Denkens*, Bern; Francke (1957) p. 59.

24. W. Friedman, *Law in a Changing Society*, London; Penguin (1964) p. 378.
25. J. Valkhoff, *Een eeuw rechtsontwikkeling*, Amsterdam; De Arbeiderspers, (1949) p. 192.
26. F. James Davis, *Society and the Law*, Law in operation, New York; The Free Press of Glencoe (1961) p. 89.
27. M. Zelditch Jr., Some methodological problems of field studies, *American Journal of Sociology*, Chicago; University of Chicago Press (March 1962) vol. 67.
28. J. H. Oosters, *Attitude verandering bij co-assistenten psychiatrie*, Amsterdam (1972) p. 4.
    G. W. Allport, The Concept of Attitude, in M. Jahoda, N. Warren, *Attitudes*, London; Penguin (1966).
29. J. Van Houtte, *Rechtsbewustzijn, een rechtstheoretisch begrip, Publieke opinie, een sociologisch begrip*, Stencil Antwerp, 1972.
30. P. Vinke, I. J. Berghuis- Van der Wijk, W. J. M. Brand-Koolen, *Houding ten aanzien van enkele aspecten van belastingheffing*, Rijksuniversiteit Leiden (1970).
31. Ranulf, *Moral Indignation and Middle Class Psychology*, New York; Schocken Books (1964).
32. For determining rigidity we asked 16 questions of the Rough-Sanford Rigidity Scale. For severity we asked 16 questions about severity against criminals.
33. J. Stone, *Social Dimensions of Law and Justice*, London; Stevens and Sons (1966) p. 324.
34. J. Habermas, *Theorie und Praxis*, Neuwied; Luchterhand (1969) p. 23.
35. P. A. Baran and P. M. Sweezy, *Monopoly Capital*, London; Penguin (1970) p. 152.
36. ibid. P. Vinke a.o. *Houding ten aanzien van enkele aspecten van belastingheffing*.
37. R. M. Titmuss, *Income distribution and Social Change*, London; George Allen and Unwin (1962) p. 17.
38. E. M. Schur, *Crimes without Victims*, New Jersey; Prentice-Hall (1965).
39. A. Mischerlich, *Auf dem Weg zur Vaterlosen Gesellschaft*, Munchen; Piper (1963) p. 154.

PUBLIC OPINION OF THE LAW IN A DEMOCRATIC SOCIETY

Wolfgang Kaupen

The question of the public's relationship to the law and its institutions is closely connected with the position of the legal system in a democratic society. For the legal system of the authoritarian state the problem was reduced to the relationship, which for the state was of general validity, between rulers and ruled, between those who gave orders and those who obeyed. A crisis of authority, i.e. questioning the claim to sovereignty, was excluded by definition: the only possibility was submission to official orders. Insubordination automatically led to a repressive reaction by the power apparatus of the state.

An analysis of the legal system of the Federal Republic of Germany shows that the dilemma of 'authoritarian state or democracy'[1] has not yet been solved. Both the self-assurance of the West German judiciary and the organizational structure of the legal system are still dominated by authoritarian standards. The process of democratising the legal system is only making hesitant progress, and is dependent on a large amount of popular and political support. In a democratic society the legal system as much as other institutions must be prepared for public criticism, though this of course goes against its own image of a professional group standing above any discussion. Neither the legal practitioner nor the jurist is used to wondering whether the present system of law perhaps ignores the needs and interests of the public. The question of the public's relationship to the law and its institutions has so far not been recognized as a relevant problem by jurisprudence. The bases of the German (but not only of the German) system of law are predemocratic. Because of their high level of abstractness, detached from social reality, they have not kept pace with changes in the social infrastructure. This is certainly not considered by members of the legal profession, by whom the discrepancy between society

43

and the administration of justice is rather regularly turned into a rebuke to society. Thus in legal literature we read now and then of an 'alarming ignorance of the law' or of an 'apathetic lack of interest' in the law and the legal system.[2] The jurist is as unaware that such an interest and a corresponding knowledge can only be developed when incentives are provided as he is unaware of most of the developments in the social sciences over the last few decades.

The sociology of law, as the science of the relationships between law and society, has in this situation a multiple task: it must analyse and criticize the theoretical system of jurisprudence (critique of ideology); it must analyse the actual system of law administration (critique of institutions); it must analyse the system of values and norms of society in relation to what is required of the administration of law and check this for consistency; it must provide jurists with the relevant sociological knowledge and, finally, it must contribute towards working out an adequate theory of jurisprudence. Public opinion research is here in no way aiming to replace the law by the 'vox populi'. Rather, it is a question of clarifying what lies behind popular attitudes to the law and its institutions and thereby creating an empirical basis for reforms that may prove necessary. How far-reaching these reforms will have to be depends on the result of the analysis. If, for example, it could be proved that the whole way the administration of law is organized does not correspond to the requirements of a democratic society, then the most plausible (political) consequence of this observation would be to formulate a radical alternative to the existing system.[3] On the other hand, if the analysis came to the conclusion that the present legal system is basically reasonable and efficient, then proposals for reforms could be formulated which were restricted to minor defects.

In order to obtain some initial indications about the relationship of the public to the law and its institutions in the Federal Republic of Germany—a topic about which there is a complete lack of empirical data—the Working Group on Sociology of Law at Cologne University carried out a representative public opinion poll in the summer of 1970. The project was stimulated by similar surveys in other European countries. The questionnaire was to some extent designed according to studies in Poland (A. Podgorecki), Denmark (B. Kutchinsky), The Netherlands (P. Vinke), and France (D. Kalogeropoulos). Our study was financed by the

German Research Foundation.

The sample comprises 1,098 adult (at least 18 years old) persons and is a disproportionately stratified random sample, housewives being under-represented by half. Besides the random sample, an additional sample of 100 'upper class' persons has been selected in order to have a sufficient number of cases for cross-tabulations with the class variable. The questionnaire was first tested in 50 interviews which enabled us to eliminate a number of questions which did not discriminate enough in the answers: when about 90% of the respondents give the same information, there is no room left for further correlation analysis, though it may be interesting for some other reasons to have even such restricted data on the degree of information among the public. But as this survey was intended to produce data for an *analytical* study, and not for a *description* of knowledge and opinion about the law, those questions with high response 'uniformity' were excluded after the pretest. The questionnaire finally included 168 questions. The interview took about 80 minutes on average, though with considerable variations either way.

A crucial point of the inquiry concerned the question as to what in fact the public appreciates as being deviant behaviour or behaviour that produces conflict, i.e. what problems are in fact passed on to the courts to be resolved. What we are dealing with here is the problem, as important as it is difficult, of the relationship between norms of the law and those outside it, especially the relationship between law and morality. Theories of jurisprudence tend to treat the normative claim of the law in isolation from the behaviour of the public and from the normative bases of this behaviour. Non-legal norms only put in an appearance if legal norms do not yet or no longer have validity for a particular field. The lawyer then speaks of 'common law'—a term that is much too undifferentiated for the large number of non-legal norms. It is not possible here to go into details of the differences between customs, mores, morals and conventions. The relevance of these distinctions would have to be investigated within the framework of a theory of social control. For the purposes of our investigation, the non-legal norms of behaviour will be called simply morals and contrasted with the corresponding legal norms. In this way we can start off with a 'moral' norm that is concerned fundamentally with conduct in regard to the law. To measure this we used the statement:

45

'You should obey the laws, even if you do not think that they are just.'

This question was answered affirmatively without qualification by the majority of the German population, viz. 66%, while 24% disagreed slightly and only 9% firmly rejected the statement.

The significance of this result, which showed hardly any changes in a series of breakdowns according to the demographic characteristics of the respondents, becomes clear if it is compared with other investigations (Table 1).

TABLE 1 : *Basic attitudes towards the law in Poland, Holland, and West Germany.*

Question (Statement)		Poland[5]	Holland[6]	Germany
The law should always be obeyed even if, in your opinion, it is wrong.	Agree	45%		
Do you think a law should be obeyed, even when you feel this law is unjust?	Yes		47%	
You should obey the laws, even if you do not think that they are just.	Agree			66%

From this it would seem as if in fact—as is often presumed—the German public is still very strongly attached to state authority. However, it should not straightaway be assumed that this 'abstract' attitude is necessarily also the attitude in a concrete situation. If this were the case then all legally prescribed or proscribed behaviour would have to be carried out without regard to opposing 'moral' norms. We attempted to examine possible variations by asking the interviewees to state in 15 cases whether the behaviour described was against the law or not, what they thought of the behaviour in moral terms, and what punishment they would give in each case if they were the judge. If the real attitude were determined by the norm that laws must be obeyed at any price, then the evaluation of behaviour not conforming to the law and the readiness to pronounce negative sanctions against such offenders, should also vary with knowledge of the legal prohibition. Table 2 shows, however, that this is by no means the case.

From this table it is clear that there are rather considerable variations in the moral evaluation and the punishment demanded even when the same level of knowledge of prohibition applies. This is clearest in those cases in which knowledge of prohibition is identical, while moral judgement and demand for punishment exhibit

46

TABLE 2: *Knowledge, Opinion and Evaluation of Fifteen Legal Cases*

Question*	Actual legal status of specified behaviour**	Defined as 'Against the Law'	Morally evaluated as 'very bad'	Punishment	
				Jail	None
		%	%	%	%
1. A workman takes 500 DM worth of materials from his firm.	×	99	37	16	2
2. A driver sees an accident and drives on without attending to the injured.	×	94	83	28	1
3. Someone does not inform the police about a planned bank robbery.	×	89	60	21	3
4. Students hold a party and smoke hashish there.	×	89	52	24	5
5. A man seduces a 15-year-old girl who does not object.	×	89	49	44	11
6. Someone moves house without registering.	×	84	4	—	27
7. A businessman transfers capital to a foreign country to avoid taxes.	(×)	69	39	37	11
8. A mother allows her son to sleep with his girlfriend in her home.	×	69	16	7	37
9. A workman has a weekend job and doesn't declare this income for taxation.	×	69	4	1	26
10. Demonstrators block rush-hour traffic.	(—)	59	20	12	17
11. A man has homosexual relations with another man.	(—)	50	28	13	40
12. A woman has an affair with a friend of her husband's.	(—)	49	28	6	26
13. A man beats up his wife because she is a bad housekeeper.	×	45	30	6	17
14. A chemist sells contraceptive pills to a 15-year-old girl.	—	31	13	2	54
15. Someone attempts suicide.	—	30	38	1	47

* The situations were described in some what more detail on the questionnaire.
** An '×' means that the behaviour is against German law; a dash '—', that it is not. Brackets indicate that the liability to punishment was recently lifted or that the legal situation is not clear.

considerable differences. But divergences are also found here between moral judgement and the demand for punishment. It would normally be assumed that the demand for punishment would vary directly with the moral evaluation, but in cases 3–5, an inverse relationship is to be observed. The proportion of respondents who plead for a jail sentence rises here with a *decreasing* moral condemnation, and simultaneously, an increasing polarization is to be observed in the demand for punishment. This result suggests that the general question about moral evaluation also is too undifferentiated to evaluate adequately the various dimensions of morality. Thus the sexual sphere has apparently a quite different value position in morality from the field of economic activity or even the field of formal administrative regulations, the violation of which is hardly seen as a moral problem. The least inclination to pronounce any negative sanction at all for behaviour that is prohibited by law is in the field of the family, which is anyway normally regulated by quite different mechanisms of social control from fields with less direct and intensive interaction. The behaviour of the mother (a serious case of procuring), who allows her adult son to sleep with his (also adult) girl-friend in her home, is even today occasionally punished by courts in the Federal Republic—according to a law that has long become obsolete, not only in the opinion of legal experts, but also as shown by the results of the questionnaire, in the eyes of the public. The change in views is expressed most clearly in the age structure: whereas a quarter of the respondents aged over 50 still expressed considerable moral objections (very bad) to the behaviour of the mother, this fraction falls to 8% among those under 35. But the proportion of those who think that this form of 'procuring' is in any case prohibited goes down simultaneously from 73% to 64%. This is an indication that the 'knowledge' itself (or more correctly, the supposition) of legal prohibition depends on the moral judgement.

If, following this, the respect for legal norms—beyond the fundamental bond to the law—depends chiefly on 'moral' norms, then it can be assumed that the attitude of the law is different among individual sections of the population. We have already been able to demonstrate this with the example of the age groups; in what follows this relationship will be pursued a little further using the respondents' preferences for particular political parties—in the assumption that the preference is at any given time the expression of a definite world and social view.

For reasons of sufficient numerical distribution we can only compare the sympathizers of the two big parties of the Federal Republic with one another: the supporters of the Christian Democratic Union (CDU/CSU) and of the Social Democratic Party of Germany (SPD).[7] To identify the two sides rather more closely some 'demographic' features will firstly be stressed. These are relevant for an investigation of attitudes to the extent that such attitudes are formed on the basis of specific socio-cultural, i.e. environmentally determined, influences. Demographic data that demonstrate such environmental influences can therefore themselves already contain some information about a person's attitudes. It can be seen, for example, that SPD supporters more frequently live in large towns, particularly in towns with more than 500,000 inhabitants, while CDU supporters are drawn more from small towns, particularly from those with less than 5,000 inhabitants. SPD supporters are found more among men, CDU supporters mainly among non-working women. The SPD attracts mainly those who receive medium incomes (800 to 1,500 DM), that is to say skilled workers, the medium range of civil servants and salaried employees. The reservoir of CDU supporters is drawn especially from those who have been to technical and secondary modern schools, from the 50–60 year age groups, and in particular from members of the Catholic church, whereas among SPD supporters Protestants and younger respondents (aged under 30) are dominant. A distinct distinguishing feature of the two 'sides', one which already approaches an attitude dimension and transcends the level of demographic features, is the question 'Would you describe yourself as an active, critical or indifferent member of your faith, or do you reject religion altogether?' Of the CDU supporters 42% described themselves as believers (SPD supporters 17%) and 31% as critical (SPD 37%). In the indifferent and rejecting categories the SPD supporters were also ahead (37% against 24% among CDU sympathizers).

The next step is to work out further differences between the supporters of the two competing parties, namely in their attitudes towards 'state and society'. From the preceding results it can already be assumed that CDU supporters are more positive and uncritical towards existing social relations or traditional structural patterns of society than supporters of the SPD, who have moreover

49

contested the traditional contents of the Christian religion to a considerably greater degree than their political opponents.

In fact with the question about their interest in politics SPD supporters already show themselves to be well ahead (43% *very* interested as compared with 33% of CDU supporters), which is also apparent in their readiness to defend themselves against an unjust administrative measure. Respondents sympathizing with the CDU indicated relatively more frequently that they would do nothing in such a situation, while SPD supporters would show stronger solidarity with their neighbours and defend their rights collectively. This readiness to participate actively, using democratic methods, in political disputes also finds expression in another question: whether 'in your opinion radical parties should be prohibited in the Federal Republic ... or should the public be allowed to decide at the elections?' 41% of CDU supporters said they should be prohibited, but only 26% of SPD sympathizers. This result may in any case come from the fact that the ban on radical parties is normally associated with the Communist Party and that the ideological contrast to Communism is much stronger among CDU supporters than among SPD supporters. This kind of association is indicated too by the results of a scale of attitudes, in which the respondents were asked to indicate their attitude to 13 groups of people and institutions in society. The scale, whose average values

TABLE 3: *Popular attitudes to groups and institutions.*

	SPD Supporters		CDU Supporters	
	Rank order	Value	Rank order	Value
Police	1	3·2	1	3·0
Lawyers	2	3·6	3	3·6
The Law	3	3·6	4	3·7
Politicians	4	3·8	7	4·2
Trade Unions	5	3·8	10	5·5
Civil Servants	6	4·0	5	3·7
Administrative authorities	7	4·3	6	4·1
Students	8	4·3	8	4·3
The Church	9	4·8	2	3·5
Major industrial concerns	10	5·2	9	4·5
Foreign workers	11	5·2	11	5·7
Communists	12	7·5	12	8·6
Hippies, beatniks	13	8·3	13	8·9

are given in the preceding tabulation, goes from 1 (highly regarded) to 10 (not well regarded), so that a high average value means a greater emotional distance, and a low favourable attitude.

From these results various conclusions can be drawn, though only some of the more important points will be emphasized here. What catches the attention first of all is that political attitudes have little or no effect on the evaluation of the guarantors of law and order, who moreover also consistently enjoy the highest regard. In the latter respect the only exception is the church: among SPD supporters it comes only in ninth place, already on the borderline of predominantly negative evaluations, whereas among CDU supporters it uncontestedly takes second place. Similar, though not quite so marked differences in the sequence of attitudes are produced for Politicians and Trade Unions, CDU supporters being less friendly towards these. Of course, if we look at the average values resulting where the position allotted is the same, it becomes clear that CDU supporters generally give freer rein to their aversion to marginal, i.e. unaccepted social groups (foreign workers, Communists, hippies and beatniks) than do respondents sympathizing with the SPD.

Finally, to demonstrate the background to the attitudes of the two political groupings one more question which dealt with the influence of the state in particular fields and social life may be referred to. The question was: 'Do you think that the government and local administration should have more say in these affairs (i.e. in those listed below), or should state control be reduced?' The results are compiled to give the proportions of those who recommend that the authorities should have more influence in the particular fields. The readiness to support stronger state intervention

TABLE 4: *The Demand for more State Influence.*

More state influence in:	SPD Supporters	CDU Supporters
	%	%
Health service	81	75
Professional and occupational training	77	69
Building of houses	72	61
Major industrial concerns	69	57
Banks, insurance	54	45
Agriculture	45	38
Trade unions	39	50

in important fields of society is generally pronounced, though here once again, SPD supporters provide almost throughout most of the advocates of state-controlled social reforms.

These examples should suffice to draw a rough picture of the typical ideological and socio-political attitudes of SPD and CDU supporters. According to these results, the latter seem to be more closely attached to traditional social structures and institutions and, because of this, to react allergically against any disturbance in the social order, while SPD supporters are aiming more for democratic participation in a *transformation of society*. That they think such a reform of society is necessary is also apparent from their opinion on the distribution of incomes and wealth in the Federal Republic: 31% of SPD supporters (as against 13% of CDU supporters) feel it is 'quite unjust'.

The attitudes to the 15 legal cases described vary in accordance with these ideological and socio-political differences, again clearly showing that these attitudes are rooted in morality (Table 5).

TABLE 5: *Knowledge, opinion and evaluation of 15* legal cases according to party preference.*

Question	Defined as 'against' the law'		Moral evaluation as 'very bad'		Jail suggested as punishment	
	SPD	CDU	SPD	CDU	SPD	CDU
	%	%	%	%	%	%
1. Theft of materials	99	99	44	50	14	18
4. Students smoke hashish	88	92	46	60	21	25
5. Seduction of girl	89	91	46	55	42	46
7. Tax avoidance	66	72	40	34	38	38
8. Procuring	66	74	16	17	7	9
10. Demonstration	54	65	19	18	10	15
11. Homosexuality	50	52	24	31	11	17
12. Adultery	44	54	21	30	4	6
15. Attempted suicide	27	36	36	41	—	1

* For reasons of clarity only those cases in which differences appear are listed in the table.

In order to demonstrate the relationship between a strong attachment to traditional moral norms and the attitude to legal sanctioning of deviant behaviour with another example, we contrasted those members of religious faiths who had described themselves as 'devout', with the interviewees who did not belong to any religion. (This characteristic is closely related, as already noted above, to party preference: 42% CDU supporters said that they were 'devout' Christians, against 17% of Social Democrat supporters). While the characteristic of party preference includes a series of 'secular' political calculations, confessions of faith should reflect still more clearly attachment to traditional morality and conventions.

The stronger relationship expected did in fact appear, especially in the morally-loaded sexual situations. But in order to avoid overburdening the report with individual results, only sharply contrasting values for the case of homosexuality will be given here as an example. 55% of practising Christians assumed (erroneously) that homosexuality between adult men is indictable, whereas the corresponding proportion among non-churchgoers was only 38%. A harsh moral verdict was given by 41% of the former—as against 20% of the latter—and lastly 18% of the Christians wanted to give a jail sentence, whereas among the non-religious only 12% did. That the differences expected do not stand out more clearly in the *demand for punishment* is because the difference in moral attitudes has already taken effect in deciding whether or not to pass sentence: only 29% of Christians did not want any sentence, against 62% of non-believers! The stronger attachment of the religiously convinced interviewees to traditional moral norms and, as a consequence of this conservative attitude, the more strongly pronounced repressive attitude towards deviant behaviour will be considered to have been sufficiently demonstrated here. We now want, in what follows, to go into the question of whether this rigid attitude also affects the relationship to the law and its administration.

In investigating the relationship to the law and the legal system we want to refer back to preference for political parties as an indicator for a more or less democratic view of the world. This means, an indicator which is to a greater or lesser extent tied to traditional conventions and is therefore prejudiced. With party preference we are, moreover, dealing with a variable which—more so than religious ties—is accessible to political discussion and change. If scientific analysis presents its results in a form that to a large extent prevents their political utilization, then it does away right from the start with its own social relevance, and itself removes the basis of its authority in a democratic society.[8] From these considerations we give preference to the indicator of sympathy for one of the two big parties in West Germany, the SPD and the CDU, against the indicator of religious ties, which in actual fact would reflect clearer differences in attitudes.

The results of the demand for sanctions against deviant behaviour suggest that attitudes to the law and its institutions depend at least to some extent on what function this element of society has in the eyes of the public. If law is only understood as an extension of 'morality', then differing expectations of the law and the legal system should be articulated—in consistency with the respective ideologies—among the supporters of the two parties. We have already established in the results of Table 3 that, with an abstract question, this is not the case. On the other hand the question about prohibiting extreme political parties already contained a clear indication of more repressive expectations of the legal system from CDU supporters. The hypothesis is also confirmed in another area, and moreover, in close connection with the moral evaluation of the 15 legal cases presented. The interviewees had the statement put to them: 'It's high time that the judges started doing something about the general decline in moral standards.' Of the supporters of the Christian Democratic Union, 69% agreed with this statement without reservations, as against only 49% of SPD sympathizers (on the basis of religious ties the difference amounted to as much as 71% against 36%). The expectations do not here extend only to the field of penal law; on the contrary CDU supporters want, for example, to tighten up the already very strict divorce laws as well (CDU 20%, SPD 13%). Restrictive norms dominate the traditional picture of the world and society, extending to concepts about adequate means of regulating behaviour. This in reply to a question about the 'main purpose served by punishment, the predominant answer is: deterrence of criminals (CDU 39%, SPD 31%).

In order to put this last result into a cross-cultural comparison, corresponding results from the Polish survey (already quoted in Table 1), and from a Norwegian[9] survey will be presented (Table 6). This shows clearly that the assumption of the deterrent effect of punishment, long scientifically disproved, generally still has most supporters in Germany, while in Poland as well as in Norway *re-education* (treatment) comes to the fore. This comparison must however, be looked at with caution, because the questions and the

TABLE 6: *Opinion on the Function of Punishment in Poland, Norway and West Germany.*

Question (Statement)*	Poland	Norway	West Germany	
			SPD	CDU
	%	%	%	%
The main aim of sentencing criminals should be:				
to re-educate them (treatment)	34			
to deter (deterrence)	22			
When the courts decide what is to be done with a law-breaker they may emphasize various viewpoints. Which point is in your opinion of most importance? Treatment		28		
Deterrence		22		
What do you think is the main purpose served by punishment? Treatment			24	20
Deterrence			31	39

* The rest of the interviewees mentioned other functions, such as 'protection of society', 'retaliation', or 'atonement'.

possible alternative answers differ considerably in the three studies referred to. However, the tendency indicated by the results gains further plausibility if the problem of deterrence is related to attitudes about the death penalty—in the (again erroneous) assumption that the death penalty has a deterrent effect. 65% of CDU sympathizers and 54% of SPD supporters believe in the deterrent effect of harsh penalties. Support for the death penalty varies accordingly (Table 7), the West German public as a whole again giving considerably higher values than the neighbouring countries.

Expectations of the law and of the legal system are clear in this basic attitude. Any means is acceptable for preserving (or restoring) law and order. Even bringing back the death penalty or, for some young people, corporal punishment (CDU 36%, SPD 27%) has a place, under these circumstances, in the body of legally available repressive measures. Equally, regard for the representatives of law and order goes up correspondingly as order is conceived in repressive terms: 63% of CDU sympathizers, as against 54% of SPD supporters, described the police—following a well-

TABLE 7: *Opinion on death penalty in Poland, Holland and West Germany.*

Question (Statement)	Poland	Holland	West Germany	
			SPD	CDU
	%	%	%	%
Do you think that death sentence should be used? On the whole yes	33			
definitely yes	16			
Capital punishment is necessary in our legal system. yes		27		
The death penalty should be brought back for certain crimes. yes			46	57

The data from the Polish sample probably differ somewhat because of an additional alternative in the answer.

known public relations slogan—as 'friends and helpers'. The closeness felt towards the police corresponds, inversely of course, to the feeling of distance from those who challenge law and order. Criminals must be treated harshly and any 'liberalization' in the execution of sentences (which, in any case, so far only exists on paper in West Germany) is rejected, as support for the following statement shows: 'The way our prisons are run these days, punishment could soon become a reward' (CDU 38%, SPD 29%). The rejection of rehabilitation measures is carried over into the personal sphere, as shown by answers to the question: 'If you were an employer would you employ a man with a prison record?' This was answered positively by only 32% of CDU sympathizers in comparison with 41% of SPD supporters.

We want next to go into the question of how this syndrome of repressive attitudes affects the relationship of the respondents to the legal system in general, i.e. including civil law. Indeed, it must here first of all be pointed out that the public is frequently unaware of the differences between civil and criminal law. Indeed, defeat in a civil dispute is not infrequently regarded as comparable with criminal sentence; the two cases have at least an approximately equal immoral content. It would therefore not be surprising under these circumstances if the expectations of conservatives with respect to criminal law were carried over to other branches of the law. This might, for example, work out in such a way that the conservative

56

respondents shun contact with the (criminal) law. The results, in fact, point to such a tendency. Thus, while the location of nearly all the various kinds of courts was better known to supporters of the CDU than to those of the SPD, the latter had themselves more often 'had something to do with the court'. The difference arises mainly from the SPD supporters having had more frequent *voluntary* contact (e.g. 'as a spectator in the public gallery'), in other words not from their being more liable to be charged with an offence.

The conservative respondents draw their knowledge of the law, to which they attribute mainly a retributive function, all the more often from second hand sources. A question relevant to this showed which problems especially are of chief interest and therefore attract attention: CDU supporters had more frequently heard, read or seen on television something about criminal procedures during the past few weeks (CDU 41%, SPD 37%),[10] while reports about Nazi trials had relatively more frequently caught the eyes of SPD supporters (18%, CDU 13%). While it is true that the latter are also criminal procedures, they have however—in the minds of the respondents, too—a quite different significance from, for example, housebreaking or a current case of bodily injury. These, it can be agreed, do more to prejudice a conservative citizen's feeling of security than do cases of long past Nazi crimes, which—as was frequently argued some years ago—after such a long time it would be 'better to let rest'.

The fact that conservatives obtain their information from secondary sources means that they are also not so well informed about the detailed organization of the courts. For example, CDU supporters more frequently mixed up the tasks of judge, prosecutor and defence counsel in a trial. In addition, as regards the function of the defence counsel, it was demonstrated that for CDU supporters this tended to mean the *defence* of the accused in a criminal procedure, while among SPD sympathizers the *advisory* function of the counsel was also taken into consideration. There was also a difference in the answers of the two groups of respondents in relation to their appreciation of the qualities of judges and prosecutors. CDU supporters tended to give a more positive evaluation on a scale between positive and negative characteristics, when they did not fall back on neutral average values. The latter could also be observed in answer to the question: 'Do you think that German courts tend on the whole to be too strict or too lenient with defendants?' Here too, CDU supporters tended towards the middle, namely to give the answer 'just right'. Apart from this, though, the proportion of those demanding tougher sentences was also preponderant (CDU 42%, SPD 35%).

This *tendential* criticism by the conservatives does not in fact significantly affect confidence in the legal system, as at another point in the questionnaire the question was asked, whether it would be better if courts were made up of ordinary citizens instead of lawyers and barristers, etc. In answer 55% of CDU sympathizers, but only 49% of SPD supporters, expressed themselves in favour of the courts being staffed with professional lawyers, whereas the vote for a mixed staffing tended in the opposite direction. It is true that these differences are not very marked, however they all point in the same direction, namely to a less critical (because less informed) attitude among the conservative CDU supporters towards the administration of the law. Thus, among supporters of the CDU in answer to the question: 'You sometimes hear that lawyers make things more complicated than they are. Do you think that this is true?' 48% said that the statement was *false,* while only 42% of SPD sympathizers shared this view. On the other hand and suggesting that the conservative respondents' confidence in the administration of the law is not so stable as it outwardly appears, in a civil dispute CDU supporters would more often prefer to reach an agreement outside the courts, the reason given being that the costs of proceedings were too high. That this is a very threadbare excuse behind which is hidden a more basic lack of identification, is suggested by a further question, where the costs of proceedings had to be estimated. Here it was shown that only 7% of the CDU supporters had estimated the costs anywhere near correctly (against 15% of SPD supporters)—most of the estimates being only *one third* of the real costs!

It is possible that it is because of the far-reaching ignorance about the real level of legal costs that the (less critical) CDU sympathizers hold less often than SPD supporters the view that a lot of money can influence the verdict. The connection between financial power and treatment in court must not, of course, be reduced to the problem of 'corruption'. Rather, the main point is that advice and representation by a 'good' (i.e. a successful) lawyer is hardly, for the average citizen, financially attainable. That a good lawyer *can* influence considerably the outcome of a trial was undisputed by 95% of all respondents. All the same, only 38% of CDU supporters answered the question: 'Do you think it is easier to get a favourable verdict if you have got a lot of money?' with an unqualified 'Yes'. Among SPD supporters the proportion came to 47%. But, besides the question of financial inequality, the respondents also felt that treatment in court showed social discrimination. This was expressed in the answers to the question: 'Do you think that an ordinary man isn't treated as well in court as a man who is better off?' 35% of CDU sympathizers (against 47% of SPD supporters) thought there was discrimination, and the reason given for this was, especially among CDU supporters, differences in social status. Discrimination in court against the 'ordinary man' is, in any case, something which he himself is more likely to notice, whereas the majority of 'better situated' people deny this inequality of opportunity. 43% of respondents with a secondary school education assume that treatment in court is unequal, against only 28% of respondents with a higher education. This difference in attitudes could be interpreted to mean that, in any given case, those who profit from a settlement do not recognize (or do not want to recognize) the unjustness of the settlement. Those who are economically well-situated dispute that their financial power also obtains privileges for them in court. Those who are favoured by their social status do not see the barriers (which, among other things, go right into the linguistic sphere) that a member of a discriminated group in society must overcome if he is to claim his formally equal rights. Finally, those who have retained a conservative image of themselves and of society (e.g. CDU sympathizers) can only imagine with difficulty that members of other social strata have basically lower chances of obtaining justice with the help of the courts. Their good conscience can even be appeased by noting that in fact offences against what is written in the laws happen more frequently among members of the under-privileged strata of the population. Of course, this overlooks the fact that regulations are determined with a one-sided regard for interests, that observing the behaviour of members of society is selective according to their social status, and finally that even the same behaviour can be differentially interpreted.

The sociology of law has so far only just begun to investigate this distortion within the legal system of the processes of perception and evaluation. It is true that extensive studies in various countries about the bias towards recruiting lawyers from the middle class are available, but there is so far only some initial information about how the biased moulding of the lawyer's personality by a definite social environment affects his professional attitude. In this connection lawyers themselves tend to point to their very small scope for personal valuation, since they are after all 'bound to the law'. This view of themselves does not correspond to reality. Being bound to the law only means that decisions are taken within a certain framework, whereas familiarization with the facts and background of the case to be judged, and its interpretation too, already leave a wide scope for personal judgement. It is possible that the fear of bias in a single judge caused the more open-minded respondents (SPD sympathizers) to favour a big rather than a small bench (20%, against 13% of CDU supporters), on the assumption that on a big bench the counterbalance of other judges prevents possible errors of interpretation on the basis of personal prejudices. We cannot decide here whether the replies of the respondents proceeded from this consideration; still less can we examine, on the basis of the material available, whether a corporate bench is able to prevent the erroneous decisions of a single judge. From the information already presented it may also be the case that, on a larger bench, the pressure from his colleagues to conform tends rather to commit the individual judge to professional conventions and norms which are much less tailored to bringing about justice in the individual case than to the security and order of the legal system itself.

We must also interpret the existing procedural forms of the courts from the point of view of making judicial activities easier, and not so much as an essential element in 'getting to the truth'. Discussion about the traditional formality of the courtroom flared up in West Germany some time ago around marks of judicial authority such as the raised bench and the judge's robe and cap. In conformity with these insignia of the 'dignity' of the court, the public—and of course the parties, especially the accused—must rise when the judge enters or leaves the courtroom. The reaction of an angry young man (with the descriptive name of Fritz Teufel, i.e. in English 'devil'), who at first refused to stand up and then did so with the comment: 'If it helps to get to the truth...' has already become proverbial. Thus far discussion about the 'dignity' of the

60

courts has already made considerable breaches in the formal authority of the legal system, and even among judges there no longer exists a united front against critics of the legal system. This transformation has similarly made a clearly visible impact on popular consciousness. In answer to the question: 'Would you prefer to take part in a trial where everybody sits together at one table, or would you prefer it if the judge sits apart on a higher level?' 42% of all respondents favoured a round-table hearing and only 36% the raised judicial bench. Yet again, the results differ here according to the ideological background of the respondents. The conservative supporters of the CDU, as many as 43%, still clung to the visible signs of official authority which, the repressive function of the law being uppermost for them, is thoroughly consistent. On the other hand only 32% of SPD sympathizers, for whom democratic rules at least tend to seem desirable in the law, still favoured the raised bench. Similar differences resulted from the question: 'Do you think that it is important for the judge and barristers to wear robes during a trial?' In this case 60% of SPD supporters were against the robing regulation, but only 45% of CDU supporters. The reason frequently given by the latter was that formality produces a more solemn, distinguished impression of the hearing, or in other words that the irrationality of the hearing, which is tied up with the repressive concepts of the conservative citizen, can be better camouflaged with robes and caps, as well as with other insignia of sovereign power.

If, with the traditional formalism of the court hearing, which is in no way limited to robing regulations, but penetrates right into the legal way of thinking and arguing, we were dealing with the attempt to construct a sham reality behind which the participants' private prejudices can then establish themselves unhindered, we now have lastly to look at a phenomenon that constitutes a direct barrier to equality before the law. This is the principle that the hearing is verbal, which in the German courts of civil law is what happens *in principle*, that is according to formality. In legal practice though, this principle is as a rule limited to noting that the briefs presented are complete. Judgement is then pronounced on the basis of a study of the documents. This procedure, which in most cases is preceded by a hortatory process for the legal recovery of a money claim, amounts to a considerable restriction in articulating their interests for the section of the public which is less practised

61

in reading and writing. It can be supposed, although there are no results of systematic investigations about this available yet, that most of the members of underprivileged sectors of the population already come a cropper in the preliminaries to the actual court hearing through failure to comply with formal requirements. Resorting to the help of a lawyer, which could bridge such information gaps, remains essentially restricted to the higher social levels. Firstly, only a third of those respondents who had been to secondary school and who had not learnt a trade, had ever sought the assistance of a lawyer (among those with matriculation the proportion rises to over two thirds). Secondly, only 11% of the members of this sector, underprivileged educationally and therefore also in not having equal opportunities (against 72% of those with matriculation), indicated that they had a lawyer among their friends or relations. Under these circumstances it is understandable that supporters of the SPD favour a democratization of the legal system and, at the same time, the principle of verbal hearings in civil law. This medium enables the interests of educationally underprivileged groups among the public to be better articulated than does the exchange of extensive briefs, especially since there is hardly any possibility in the written proceedings of bridging the gap between the highly formalized language of jurisprudence and the ordinary language of everyday life.

These problems were in any case not the object of the empirical investigation about the relationship of the West German public to the legal system. They were merely brought up in order to be able to interpret more adequately the respondents' answers to questions in this field. It was the general intention of this contribution, using statements of the public about the existing legal system, to refer to basic problems of the administration of justice in a democratic society. As the respondents' way of thinking is very strongly marked by the social structure, unchanged for decades in the field of legal administration, and since alternative models of a legal system have not so far been developed, let alone discussed, we have only been able, through observing a developing democratic consciousness (mainly among sympathizers of the German Social Democratic Party), to suggest the possibilities of a democratic administration of justice. Whether such possibilties can be realized in the Federal Republic of Germany in the foreseeable future and how, in particular, the detailed contents of a democratic legal system will be expressed are quite different matters. In this connection the issue of whether the alternatives developed in the last few years in the other part of Germany, the German Democratic Republic, can be regarded as democratic foundations of a legal system cannot be avoided. This analysis which must be approached without ideological bias, still has to be carried out. The sociology of law is at present still concerned with breaking down, through a critique of ideology, the German judiciary's traditional view of itself and thereby preparing the ground for a way of thinking that is oriented to social problems.

NOTES

1. Cf. W. Kaupen and Theo Rasehorn, *Die Justiz zwischen Obrigkeitsstaat und Demokratie* (Justice between Authoritarian State and Democracy), Neuwied; Luchterhand Verlag, 1971.
2. As, for example, in the speech of one of the most prominent German judges, Sarstedt, at a meeting of the Federal Welfare Court in 1970; a similar tendency is shown in the results of a survey of administrative judges, cf. Axel Görlitz, *Verwaltungsgerichtsbarkeit in Deutschland* (The Administrative Courts in Germany), Neuwied; Luchterhand Verlag, 1970.
3. As an example of a very far-reaching critical approach cf. Severin-Carlos Versele, 'Towards an anti-justice?' *European communications on the sociology of law*, No. 7 (April 1972).
4. The figures given below are representative of the adult population of West Germany, without taking account of the additional sample.
5. The comparative data for Poland have been taken from Adam Podgorecki 'The prestige of Law (Preliminary Research Results)' *Acta Sociologica* (10, 1966) pp. 81–96.
6. The Dutch results have been collected by P. Vinke, *Inner Acceptation of Legal Rules*, Leiden (mimeographed paper).
7. From the representative sample of the population 463 persons (39%) 'voted' for the SPD, 379 (32%) for the CDU.
8. As this way of thinking is rather unconventional according to the positivistic concept of science, some explanatory words seem to be appropriate. Sociology of law—more so than the social sciences generally—is especially exposed to the danger of losing sight of social conditions and the consequences of its activities. Drawing up and applying the law is largely a state monopoly, and scientific research can only benefit this monopoly if it does not expressly include the institutional framework of the administration of the law and its social background. If, then, sociology of law is to contribute not only to refining the administrative implements of the state—in whoever's interest this may be—but also (beyond its own 'academic' cognitive interest) to overcoming interests which are not democratically legitimated, then it must not formulate

63

research problems and results abstractly, without reference to particular, concrete, social relationships. Positivistic neutralism overlooks the fact that even ostensibly 'value free' research is connected with definite social interests and is above all 'exploited' by them. Therefore the scientist who retreats to the apparently unpolitical territory of value free research is in reality contributing to consolidating the social status quo: he produces establishment knowledge! If, however, science cannot be carried out in a social vacuum, which therefore also means not in a value free way, then it must be possible to demand of a scientist that he should make the 'political' background to his activities clear and visible. Only in this way can he fulfil the scientific demand of the greatest possible rationality and objectivity.

9. Cf. Berl Kutchinsky 'Law and Education: Some Aspects of Scandinavian Studies into "The General Sense of Justice" ', *Acta Sociologica* (10, 1966) pp. 21–41.

10. These differences of a few per cent are not significant in the statistical sense. We have quoted them nevertheless, as, taken altogether, they tend in the direction of the hypothesis put forward, and in a more exact measurement of 'ideology' (e.g. using the indicator of religious ties) it is highly probable that the differences would be much more prominent. For basic reasons we have not given a calculation of tests of statistical significance; for this cf. e.g. Johan Galtung, *Theory and Methods of Social Research*, Oslo 1967.

11. This is confirmed by the participant observation study which was carried out recently by Rudiger Lautmann in higher German courts. Cf. R. Lautmann, *Justiz—Die stille Gewalt* (Justice—The Secret Power) Athenaum Verlag; Frankfurt 1972.

PUBLIC OPINION ON LAW*

Adam Podgorecki

Lawyers and legal scholars educated in the spirit of dogmatic legalism, in the civil, penal or administrative spheres, believe that law is defined by its validity, or by its being enacted by the authorized state agencies. They do not seem to be concerned by the obviously tautological nature of such a position. Indeed, if law is whatever is valid, while what is not so, is not law, a question arises: upon what principle is validity itself based. Those who are prepared to ignore the tautology would answer that whatever is valid is so because it is law. Some of the more scrupulous dogmatic lawyers would modify this position somewhat by saying that whatever is valid is so because an authorized power has so enacted. But authorized on what principle? On a legal one, is the retort. Thus the tautology reappears though its circumference is greater.

The problem of the validity of law is a complex one and, as might be expected, several positions may be adopted. Positive or valid law may be distinguished from that which is non-positive; statute law may be distinguished from the intuitive or 'vivid' legal sentiments, from public awareness[1], and from common law (though the latter causes further difficulty in so far as it is sometimes subsumed under what is enacted and sometimes not). However without entering into semantic disputes at this time (the debate seems particularly arid because of the *a priori* assumptions underlying the respective positions) one point should be noted. The concept of law as limited to what has been legitimately enacted is too narrow for the analysis of the 'social efficiency' of legal measures. And such a concept, apart from its being theoretically fallacious, can lead to a number of undesirable practical consequences.

There are occasions when there is a discrepancy between positive law and legal awareness. If the legislature enacts a bill which does

* Mr Piotr Graff of Warsaw University assisted greatly in translating the text from Polish and I am indebted to him.

not coincide with the prevailing legal feelings of society, it must expect resistance promoted by those feelings. The greater the conflict between such feelings and the proposed law, the more difficult will be its enforcement. The legislature may force such a bill through, but then the social costs will increase accordingly. Laws which are compatible with social sentiments do not face such obstacles and hardly need enforcement. Such kinds of legal measures may be said to be cheap. Sometimes, however, a legislature may be aware that a bill is incompatible with some social sentiment or other and it will consequently be prepared to resort to more drastic measures of enforcement. But such a decision should rest upon what are thought to be particularly important political or social principles.

A legislature which attempts to use the law to introduce new values into a society will encounter resistance indicative of the struggle between new statute laws and old legal feelings. In such situations, a calculation of the eventual social profits and losses is quite essential. The legislature will consider as profits all the planned consequences of the efficient application of the new law, and as losses all hindrances and obstacles (such as court actions, faulty running of the administrative apparatus, attempts to out-wit the law, and social resistance to the new law) which may result from the continued acceptance of former legal feelings.

The above description however obviously assumes that the legislature acts rationally, proceeds with the necessary knowledge, and is conscious of the actual distribution of gains and losses. Reality however rarely lives up to such an ideal. It is the task of science and of the sociology of law in particular to inform the legislature to what extent the proposed law is likely to be obeyed, the strength of support it will find in prevailing legal feelings, and what discrepancies will eventually appear between the new law and former legal feelings. It should then be the responsibility of the legislature to calculate the costs of the introduction of the law, in terms of undesirable effects and the importance of the projected or intended objectives and values. It is not the job of scientists to take the legislature's decisions, but it is their duty to warn it about possible mistakes and to provide it with data enabling it to act on adequate evidence rather than guesswork, intuition or sudden revelation.

Legal systems in every society seek to have universal application.

And there is a unity in the legal system (though it can deal differentially with different classes or groups) to the extent that it assumes there are no insoluble cases—that is that there are no problems which do not come within its regulatory control. This tendency towards unity or universality is by no means limited to 'valid law'; it is also typical, though to a lesser degree, of the 'legal sentiments' of societies. The above feature is peculiar to law and is not to be found in other fields. For example from surveys on the choice of career, leisure activities or consumer habits, it is known that there are many factors which tend to differentiate opinions. Public opinion on such issues is heterogeneous being dependent on such factors as education, occupation, income, sex and social status. However, where views concerning the law are involved, the situation is different. Legal prescriptions are not subject to individual decisions and legal systems are often maintained over many generations. There is no general acceptance of the view that legal prescriptions can be chosen at will, or that many different legal systems should be introduced into a given society. Thus there is a general demand for uniformity of the system of law and for a similar uniformity of the legal sentiment throughout the society.

In this connection a fundamental problem arises which can be reduced to the question: is there such a thing as the legal sentiment of a society? The issue is a difficult and complex one. Indeed, can the sum of individual responses, even if they are all consistent, be understood as the fixed view of the whole society? Would the votes in a poll on what law should be like, really reflect the views of the members of the society? Or would they perhaps be different if we asked for an uncommitted opinion without any consequences, or if those questioned answered after calm consideration of complicated arguments pertaining to legal issues? Would the answers be different if they were declared after a discussion compelling people to take sides? How differently would people reply when there were for them practical consequences of their answers from when there were no such consequences? All these doubts are mentioned to point out the essential fact that a man asked about his opinion on a certain matter (and this is particularly true with respect to legal issues) usually responds as a person who is not interested in the actual answer and, moreover, as a person who can have no influence on the issue at stake.

This is not a problem which can be ignored particularly since it is not at all easy to explain what is meant empirically when we talk about the legal sentiments of a society. Is it the legal sentiment of social and political leaders, or of the intelligentsia or of the working people or of the man in the street? Alternatively does the term refer to the arithmetical majority of the population?

When we attempt to investigate legal sentiments, we must be aware of such problems. Thus the subject matter of the study should be emotionally important for the respondents, but on the other hand it should not involve their interests in such a way as to produce a tendency towards systematic bias in their answers. It also should not produce feelings of inferiority in the respondent. However an investigation of legal sentiments ought to concern problems which are not too remote from the everyday experience of the respondents; and the problem selected for study must be amenable to presentation in simple everyday language.

Studies on Parental Authority

It seems that parental authority is an appropriate issue to focus on in a survey of public opinion. Two research projects in this area will be reported on: one American and one Polish.

The main aim of the American researchers was to investigate the following problems:

(a) what are the consistencies and inconsistencies between the laws concerning parental authority and the society's legal sentiments on this issue?

(b) are these sentiments uniform throughout the population, or are they fragmented?

(c) what, if any, is the influence of such factors as age, income, sex, education and religion upon the views concerning law?

(d) what motives and reasons are relied on by people in justifying their views on parental authority?

(e) to what extent do the results of sociological investigations justify the soundness of alternative legal prescriptions?[2]

The sample studied was randomly chosen from the population of adult inhabitants of the State of Nebraska (with the exception of persons detained in mental asylums and prisons). It was decided that one person per thousand adult inhabitants would be interviewed and this yielded a total sample of 860. The questionnaire took 13 months to prepare and was modified after two pilot studies. The sample was stratified on the following factors: rural or urban residence, race, nationality, income, number and age of children, social status, education, sex, age, occupation, religion and membership of associations and trade unions. Upon examination the sample turned out to be representative of the general population in terms of these variables.

The results of the research allow us to formulate some general opinions concerning the views on parental authority as expressed by the respondents in the American sample. Parental authority is defined by the real sentiment of the community to the child's advantage. Older views, construing parental authority as an authoritarian institution, occasionally based on a belief in the 'natural rights' of parents towards children, do not find many adherents. The research suggests that parental authority is seen as a means to certain pedagogical aims rather than as an end in itself. And it appears that the general public would not resent intervention by the law if it also provided facilities for the better upbringing and education of children. It is apparent too, that the general opinion tends to accept more autonomy for the child than the law actually grants.

Apart from conclusions that may seem to be instrumental or topical concerning the scope or content of parental authority, the study also suggests more general questions. In trying to explain why there is such a large discrepancy between legal sentiments and the positive law, it was found that family law is not exposed to any particular pressure group activities. As is well known American legislatures are vulnerable to the influence exerted by various social and political vested interests represented by pressure groups.[3] The better organized more affluent and more active groups can often gain advantages (the values sought to be furthered by groups seem of secondary importance). The fact that there is a remarkable inconsistency between the positive law and the legal sentiments concerning parental authority, its structure, powers and scope, may be in part accounted for, according to the researchers, by the lack of appropriate pressure groups.

As we know, in American law, the system of precedent is highly developed and judges are apt to be intensely attached to authority in expounding and administering the law. Established procedures are strongly resistant to change, and in comparison with other types of case there are relatively few law suits concerning family law matters. Conflicts between parents and children rarely end up in court. And, since cases are few, so are briefs, decisions, appeals and discussions of the issues. Other legal problems there-fore vie for the legislature's attention while there are few occasions where court verdicts concerning the relationship between parent and child highlight problem areas.

These considerations lead to a general hypothesis to the effect that the efficiency of the working of legal precepts is proportionate to the degree of support they find in the legal sentiment of society. This idea was formulated in rather extreme terms by Bertrand Russell who wrote: '. . . law is almost helpless if it is not supported by public sentiment, as can be seen in the United States during Prohibition or in Ireland in the 1920s, when most of the populace sympathized with the moonlighters. This is why law as a working force depends more on social support than on police power. The degree of social support for law is one of the paramount characteristics of society'.[4]

An interesting result of the investigations into parental authority is the finding emphasized by the authors that support from legal sentiment is not the only factor enhancing the efficiency of positive law. Another relevant factor is the acceptance of law through inertia. Indeed there are discrepancies between the legal sentiment and precepts concerning parental authority. However, the law works because of social inertia; conflicts requiring formal solutions do not appear because intiatives to formulate them are lacking. Inertia engenders some acceptance of the status quo.

An acceptance of law may have various origins and degrees of intensity. It can be an emotional acceptance based on a deep iden-tification of the legal sentiment with law, or it may be supported by rational considerations, or again it may result from social inertia. In each case the intensity of the acceptance enjoyed by law is apt to be different and consequently the law will be more or less res-pected. This kind of general statement, as we shall see, underlies studies of a problem which is crucial for the functioning of law: the problem of its prestige.

Research on parental authority provided valuable experience
70

of survey techniques, and it appeared to be a useful method for the analysis of the extent of acceptance of positive law. However an important limitation of survey methods must be kept in mind. Namely it is difficult to determine the validity of the answers elicited. We cannot know the degree to which an answer is sincere or reliable. This well known limitation of the survey method (counteracted to some extent by increasing methodical refinements) calls for supplementary studies using other approaches. These should provide checks on the result of opinion surveys and tell us something of their validity and objectivity. Though of course replication of opinion surveys would also be useful, the investigation discussed above highlights many issues that deserve further exploration.

Related to the American research was a Polish survey of opinion on parental authority. It was carried out in 1963 by the *Centre of Public Opinion Studies* (Ośrodek Badania Opinii Publicznej) under the supervision of A. Podgorecki.[5] A sample was drawn representative of the adult population of the country divided into rural and city dwellers. The sample was based on information drawn from the Statistical Year Book of 1961, and out of the total sample of 3,000 a response rate of almost 90% was achieved.

The Polish survey, relying on earlier experience, focused on a limited number of issues which seemed to be most significant. One problem which had not been tackled at all by American scholars was the question of 'familiarity with the law'.

The results obtained were interesting. First of all a distinction was drawn between familiarity with legal principles and familiarity with the precept of law. By legal principles was meant norms which are consistent with the popular legal sentiment: usually they refer to the nature of basic rights and obligations and broad categories of what is allowed and forbidden. On the other hand, the precepts of law are mainly technical and procedural in character; they are concerned with the available methods for the realization of the objectives enshrined in legal principles. The results of the investigation allowed the general statement that the knowledge of legal principles was fairly good while the knowledge of precept law was rather poor.

These findings seemed to confirm the supposition that legal norms broadcast by the legislature and received by the population may be received in various ways. The norms involving legal principles

71

usually reach the people after long practical training, they fall into the realm of observation of life, of knowledge about legal events, and into a pattern of personal and family experiences. From the point of view of the legislature, an internalization of legal principles is a long and complex process. The expected outcome is an acceptance of the principles.

In the case of legal precepts the situation is different. They are most often worded in esoteric juristic terminology and they are addressed above all to the officials of the law. Such people are of course professionally trained to receive messages from the legislature—to comprehend its statements whether recent or ancient. They have mastered the skill of precise legal understanding, they have learnt how to fit separate laws into an overall pattern, and they are familiar with the procedures of application. Hence, it should be supposed by way of a general hypothesis, that the ordinary man becomes familiar with law either by a long process of internalization of legal norms which are eventually transformed into legal principles, or else by a social process involving imitation of the recurrent behavioural models of legal officials. As a result, the orientation of the citizen to the contemporary form and content of law depends less on immediate access to its sources, and more on an understanding of law from the behaviour of its officials.

The set of legal principles may be analogously represented by a map of the main highways which provide the easiest and most rapid connection between various sites. Such a map tells us how to reach a desired area. However if we want to get to a specific place, we need more detailed knowledge which can be provided by a more detailed map which informs us of the roads and pathways which supplement the system of main roads. The system of legal precept can be represented as analogous to the roads and pathways.

The Polish legal system is based on different principles from the American one. At the time of the investigation family life was regulated by the *Family Code* of 1950 as amended by the 1964 Code. However the investigations proved that the precepts of the code were essentially accepted by the community. Thus reglations concerning the age at which civil rights are granted to the young, although substantially changed from the pre-war situation, were also accepted. (An open demand by the young for civil rights seems to indicate their strong desire for such rights and their desire for early participation in social and political life. Their tendency to demand what they think is their due seems to point to the large potential energy of the younger generation even if it does not necessarily reveal itself in public, social and political activity.)

It should be remarked too that an analysis of the relationship between the respondents' education and their answers to the questions concerning the age at which civil rights should be granted to youth, revealed a very significant relationship. It was the more educated groups who tended to believe that civil rights should be granted at the age of 18, which would seem to indicate that the change in the pre-war legal principle (which had held 21 as the age of maturity) had been accepted.

A comparison of the Polish and American research findings is interesting. Opinions as to whether family members in difficulty should be supported by the family itself, or by the State, were distributed differently in Poland than in the U.S.A. For example, in Poland, when a parent was ill, rural and urban populations had different opinions as to where they thought aid should come from. Among the rural population 67·9% expected help to come from their children, and 28.4% expected it to come from the State. For the urban intelligentsia, however, 49·4% looked to their children for help, and 45·5% to the State. In the American research the findings were the opposite of this; it was the rural population who proportionately expected more help from the State. It is interesting that the traditional view, that in such emergencies the family rather than the State should provide help, is still deeply rooted in the consciousness of certain social groups in Poland. For example that group of people who live in cities, but who also have a rural background, held attitudes nearer to those of the rural population than to urbanites of at least second generation standing. 55.9% of them therefore expected to receive help from their children, and only 38·9% from the State. Such a group therefore seems more attached to the attitudes of those with whom they shared a common childhood, than to the attitudes of their new urban neighbours.

Thus the investigations carried out in Poland yielded different results from American research. The Polish country folk still believe the obligation to support family members in difficulty should be the responsibility of relations rather than the State. The following explanation is suggested. The rural population is still apt to think in terms of mutual help within the family or in the neighbourhood, rather than in businesslike terms of solving their problems by resorting to administrative agencies and institutions. This type of thinking (the data would suggest that it is also widespread among town dwellers of rural origin) leads to dependence first of all upon the narrow circle of the kin network, rather than on remote bureaucratic institutions. If we try to suggest an even broader generalization it is that a comparison of Polish and American social environments reveals that in America human interaction is dry, businesslike and marked by a rational bent to formal solution even in private and family matters, while in Poland the predominating style is more emotional and humanistic.

A hypothesis that has been advanced by the American researchers is that each sex is less likely to accept limitation of its parental authority on those issues which are of most concern to it. The American survey revealed that men were more ready to limit parental authority with respect to a child's marriage, religious and health problems, while women were more ready to accept such limitations concerning the choice of a career by a child, its income and education. Polish investigations confirmed this thesis to some degree with respect to income (men's domain) and to a lesser degree with respect to religion (women's domain). In Poland much more uniformity of opinion concerning parental authority was found however—perhaps because in this country women seem to be more equal to men not only in their formal rights but also in their actual social and economic status.

Another American finding, that people with their own children are more likely to accept limitation of parental authority than childless persons, was not confirmed. Polish data even points in the opposite direction. Again, the diversity of the two cultures might offer an explanation. Perhaps the findings that childless persons demand more parental authority is not a universally valid generalization but is relative to the peculiar social setting. According to other studies,[6] in the United States children exert a strong pressure upon their parents and hence a lenient attitude on the part of the latter simply reflects their reconciliation to this situation. In the study referred to, some cases are described where parents did not want to buy a television set, as they believed there were detrimental pedagogical effects, but eventually they had to accede to the children's demands—in particular, when the children had

74

problems at school because they were not familiar with current TV programmes. Thus views on the extent of parental authority among persons who had their own children may well be a consequence of the influence exerted by the juvenile sub-culture, as well as by the larger community. It may be expected that the differences in this respect between the Polish and American societies will tend to diminish because of the increasing claims and pressures of the juvenile sub-culture in Poland.

Both the American and the Polish studies on parental authority revealed that there was a significant tendency among people to conceive law as a single, structurally coherent pattern. It was also found that the efficiency of law is proportionate to the support it gets from legal sentiment. This kind of general statement motivated us to attempt an investigation of the paramount problem: what prestige is enjoyed by law as a social institution?

STUDIES ON THE PRESTIGE OF LAW

Questions as to the prestige of law were included in the programme of research into public opinion concerning the general appreciation of law and its functioning. Two basic problems were tackled. The first task was to establish how the Polish population in 1964 conceived of law in general, of punishment inflicted by it, and of the actual functioning of judicial institutions. The objective here was to gain diagnostic knowledge about public opinion concerning the image of law and some judicial institutions. The second task was to analyse the relationships, if any, between opinions on and attitudes towards law and various psychological and social determinants of those opinions and attitudes. A group of objective and subjective social factors was considered: among the objective ones were age, sex, education, occupation, social background, place of residence; among the subjective ones were feelings of insecurity, social adjustment, rational rather than dogmatic frame of mind, religion, etc. It was significant for the study that both types of factors, objective and subjective, were considered together to assess the degree to which they influenced opinions and attitudes towards law.

Seeking to test the essential research hypothesis the question-

75

naire was so designed as to include a number of problem areas—
such as the question of obedience to law, and of evaluating the
severity of judicial decisions. Social feelings towards certain non-
legal punishments, like flogging, were also examined. Questions
were designed to test views on various functions of punishment;
on whether an unjust law should be evaded or broken and on
whether one's superiors should be obeyed even if their orders or
demands are unsound. Finally, it was asked, on what factors
did a positive outcome of transactions with or applications to the
State agencies depend? The research was carried out in 1964 by
the *Centre of Public Opinion Studies* under the supervision of A.
Podgorecki.[7] Out of a total national sample of 3,000 adults a
94% response rate was achieved using slightly different questionnaires for the urban and rural populations. The sample was representative of the Polish population with only a slight bias in terms
of educational distribution.

The study was performed by the Centre's staff who have extensive experience in interviewing and analysing questionnaires. As a
result of two pilot studies carried out earlier by sociologists among
the most extreme populations (a village remote from urban centres
and a big city; people with higher education and the uneducated.
etc.), a revised version of the questionnaire was drafted. Considerable care was taken to ensure that the interviewers were familiar
with and fully understood the questionnaire they were using and
its purposes.

An analysis of the results of this research led to a number of
interesting and partly unexpected findings. Firstly a general conclusion was that persons who are socially well situated tend to
respect law more. The fact that frustrated persons and those who
express feelings of social insecurity made declarations against
respecting the law can be approached in two ways. The first
tentative explanation refers to the frustration–aggression hypothesis
and to the supposition that those who tend to feel more insecure
are prone to aggression against all the encountered forms and
structures of social life, and in particular against the institutions
which impose order upon social life. Another explanation assumes
that some of the frustrated and maladjusted persons are those who
do not agree with the society's legal patterns and, being so critically
minded, are apt to welcome changes. Such a frame of mind may
lead to a critical attitude towards the existing legal situation.

76

It was also discovered that in various contexts certain social or individual characteristics systematically result in more rigorous attitudes. (By this term we mean punitiveness or the tendency to select the most severe penal measures out of those available.) The following factors were associated with punitiveness: lower education, manual occupations, feeling of lack of security, social isolation, a severe upbringing, dogmatic attitudes, poor social adjustment, and feelings of frustration. On the other hand, the following factors made for a greater tolerance: high school or university level education, non-manual occupation, involvement in voluntary social service, a lack of insecurity, multiple social contacts, an appreciation of one's own childhood as lenient, rational attitudes towards problems, good social adjustment, and a lack of feelings of frustration. It is remarkable that only two of these factors (education and occupation) are objective determinants; the others are subjective in character. At first glance it might seem probable that manual workers are more rigorous in their parental attitudes because of a particular working class sub-culture, with more traditional pedagogical practices and stereotypes. Such a hypothesis would relate the greater punitiveness of manual workers to the specific norms and child rearing practices of this social group rather than to manual labour as such. However such an explanation is incompatible with the available data. Indeed it was found that manual labour acts as a factor leading to greater punitiveness also in other fields, unconnected with the peculiar pedagogical practices of the working class, e.g. with respect to theft or to general views on the function of punishment. Thus it seems more plausible to suppose that manual work is significantly related to punitive attitudes.

In analysing the influence of various factors upon punitive attitudes there might be a tendency to deny an independent role to various subjective determinants. It might be argued that since many significant relationships have been found between objective social factors and subjective ones, the influence of the latter is only an indirect consequence of the former. However, such a position calling an independent role for the subjective variables into question, would not be valid. It is disproved quite clearly by the data relating to opinions on the use of the death penalty. In this context, all the factors inducing greater punitiveness, i.e. an acceptance of capital punishment, turned out to be subjective in character. These were: insecurity feelings, a severe upbringing and poor social adjustment. It can be seen that none of the factors labelled as objective works towards greater punitiveness. Thus an independent influence from various subjective social variables has been demonstrated and thereby it has been made clear that social researches in general, and sociological investigations of the working of law in particular, should not be limited to the analysis of the traditional objective factors only.

The essential question therefore concerns the nature of the relationship between various factors inducing an indvidual either to a greater punitiveness or to a greater tolerance. Both types of factors are envisaged and the following generalization may be suggested: punitively minded persons are those marked by a narrow knowledge of individual cases and of social mechanisms, while tolerantly minded persons have a better knowledge and experience. A narrow scope of social experience is expressed in the belief, based on simple-minded observation of everyday life, that systematically punishing behaviour leads to inhibition. This principle is mechanically projected upon and into the complicated world of the interplay of social factors, with a naive belief that what is sauce for the goose is good for the gander.

A general remark can be made that if a person is faced with an example of abuse of personal authority, or if he is asked about his attitude towards theft, homicide, or an act of street violence, he will experience a feeling of repulsion or indignation which has been implanted in him by tradition; he will experience tension and will seek to relieve it. But thereafter, he has two ways to achieve a solution. If his social experience is sufficiently broad he will see the opportunity to reach for therapeutic, preventative or educative means, which might be instrumental in avoiding or limiting the negative effects of the misbehaviour. However, if he lacks such experience, he will probably tend to relieve his own tension by resorting to an emotional reaction. The response to the need to get rid of emotional tension is to inflict punishment on others. Thus, if we accept the assumption that a relieving of tension constitutes a reward, then a punishment inflicted upon someone else can constitute a reward in such a situation.

Another interesting result of our research emerges from a comparison of factors related to punitiveness with those which relate to obedience of law, compliance to superiors, and to a constructive
78

appreciation of institutions and their working. It may be seen that a number of factors which systematically intensify punitiveness, are similarly systematically conducive to the lack of obedience of law, and conversely the factors which promote tolerance also induce obedience to the law. The following factors tend to increase punitiveness in some situations and influence the lack of respect for law in others: low education, unskilled manual labour, feelings of insecurity, social isolation, a severe upbringing, dogmatic attitudes, poor social adjustment, frustration. The following factors work in the opposite direction: high school or university education, non-manual work, lack of insecurity feelings, good social adjustment, lack of frustration. The fact that the essential factors listed in each group usually tend to occur together makes us suppose that punitiveness and a lack of respect for the law are parallel phenomena. It should be expected that the validity of this hypothesis will depend on the type of society and the state of the social system in which it is tested. Very important consequences grow from these considerations; in some situations an intensification of punitiveness works towards a lowering of respect for the law, while an increase of tolerance also increases the law's prestige. Generally speaking these relationships mean that if the factors leading to punitiveness act more intensively, law will be less respected, and the converse would be true as well. Of course, this does not mean that an extreme lowering of punitiveness in some situations, or too broad limits for tolerance on some issues, cannot undermine the respect for law. What is meant, however, is a proposition extremely important in both theoretical and practical terms that within a given pattern of conditions it is better to accept a tolerant solution of problems than a punitive one. If no other important considerations prevent it tolerant solutions indirectly increase the respect for law, and their societal impact can be quite remarkable.

Sociologically interesting is the category of persons declaring a respect for law. It is the 'intelligentsia', i.e. people with high school education and beyond, coming from educated families, performing non-manual jobs (objective characteristics) and persons without feelings of insecurity, rationally minded, members of small groups and individuals actively engaged in public works (subjective determinants). Even if we take account of the more declarative character of the responses of this category of people, the fact remains that

79

it is a group of persons professionally situated to execute the law on various levels of state administration, with direct or indirect influence in various institutions. Probably it is this professional routine which, whatever the prevailing beliefs on those matters are, exerts its decisive impact upon the feelings of respect for the law in the intelligentsia.

Everyday common experience and observation would lead us to believe that the degree of obedience to law is rather moderate in the general population from which the sample was taken. Thus, it might seem quite surprising that many people (44·3% of the urban population and 45·3% of the rural population) declared that law should be obeyed unconditionally, even when it is considered to be unjust. An explanation which can be offered postulates a collective societal attitude towards law which is different from individual feelings and which may be termed Socratic. Socrates respected law even when he refused to respect the judges who administered it. His view was that law can be misused in some individual cases and contexts but that the total system should be respected in spite of any disdain for the manner in which it is administered. We can suppose that such a legalistic attitude is the result of an age-old collective experience shaped by and built up through many complex and contrasting situations. It is by no means easy to undermine the historically accumulated and treasured capital of respect for the law, developing through the centuries an inertia which resists short-lived changes and disturbances. The immediacy of events does not allow us to see this sentiment in a proper perspective—it therefore hides from us the extensive reservoir of established collective attitudes.

Our investigation also allowed us to grasp some elements of the social background behind the law. Parts of the data can be interpreted in a number of ways. For example, it can be seen that persons with uncompleted education are apt to manifest feelings of insecurity, irrational attitudes and incoherence of their system of beliefs. In this connection it can be supposed that these persons reveal some relics of the judgements, attitudes and opinions which were characteristic of the social class known as the petty bourgeoisie. Socially threatened, this class used to make its political, economic and social strivings more and more radical, giving to them a primitive, but still uniform and coherent shape, and relying on a system of beliefs which made use of rational arguments (or at least such as seemed so within several mythological or rationalizing contexts) to achieve its self-seeking objectives.

Skilled workers conceive of their childhood as punitive (this is also true of the more general category of persons with working-class backgrounds). Unskilled workers reveal a number of features which can be negatively evaluated: elements of feeling insecure, social isolation, inhibited contact with other people, poor social adjustment and a conception of their own childhood as punitive. It is not surprising that unskilled workers should hold such attitudes since advances in education and training have forced them to compare themselves with two better off reference groups. One of these groups is the skilled workers who enjoy higher social prestige, have greater job security and have grasped the opportunities for cultural and social advancement. The other group is the white collar workers. The social distance between unskilled labourers and the latter group, rather extensive previously, has become narrower. However white collar workers participate to a greater extent than manual workers in the advantages of the technological civilization and are much more able to gain benefit from the administrative apparatus.

It is remarkable that persons engaged in voluntary social activities (i.e. those who more easily accept the social reality in which they live than other people), regularly reveal a greater propensity to tolerance, and also respect law more than others. However, these persons, perhaps believing that their engagement in such activities authorizes them to be more independent in their opinions, do not appear to obey their superiors when the latter make decisions they themselves do not believe in.

A number of objections may be raised against our investigations into the prestige of law. It may be argued that responses to many of the questions put (and the interviewers were sometimes of higher social status than the respondents) are merely declarative, since nobody likes to appear a barbarian and everyone is proud of his humanitarianism. Another possible objection is that the results have not been sufficiently verified by other research methods: or that among the relationships discovered, the strategic factors have not been distinguished with sufficient clarity.

However in spite of these and other possible shortcomings, the study points out that the question of the prestige of law is an important one worthy of further investigation.

From the existing data emerges a main hypothesis which is important for further research. It is as follows—that certain classes of people are induced to respect the law, to a greater or lesser degree, by objective economic demogaphic and other such factors. But there may be other factors which play important complementary roles. We may suppose that various aspects of the working of law, like its evaluation, acceptance, internalization, the patterns of legal behaviour, etc. are modified not only by the general types of social structure, but also by the values cherished by various social groups within their respective judicial sub-cultures; within each of these groups, the extent, mode and degree of respect for the law seem to depend on personality factors.

Thus there are at least three prisms through which the abstract working of a judicial norm is refracted: the first and basic one is the type of social-economic system; the second is the judicial sub-culture to which the norm is addressed; the third is the psycho-social determinants of a personality responding to the norms.

Studies on Moral and Legal Views of Polish Society

Studies on the prestige of law provided a basis for a subsequent survey. This was a general population sample designed to examine the basic moral and legal views of Polish society.[8]

The methodological lessons learned from public opinion investigations concerning divorce, parental authority and various aspects of the prestige of law, guided the planning of the later studies into moral and legal attitudes. Thus a special emphasis was laid on personality variables, in particular those which had turned out to be important in the earlier surveys. On the other hand, the variables which had contributed little or nothing to our knowledge were abandoned, and concepts of legal punitiveness and tolerance were extended into various new fields of social activity. Supplementary projects were also undertaken, reaching beyond the main design and directed at investigating some specific judicial sub-cultures: namely, the legal and moral views of judges and recidivists.

This investigation of legal and moral views led to many new and interesting results. One of them was the finding that it was empirically justifiable to distinguish between fundamental and

82

instrumental attitudes. By fundamental attitudes is meant a disposition to accept some legal norm or precept because it deserves respect as a valid piece of law, and by instrumental attitudes is meant a tendency to accept the legal norm or precept because it is appreciated as advantageous or useful. A 'fundamentalist' reacts spontaneously without reckoning his own gains and losses. An 'instrumentalist' reacts by coldly estimating various subjectively conceived advantages and disadvantages.

Without entering into the technical details of the five questions which provided the basis for distinguishing the types of attitude, it is worth mentioning that they were mutually correlated, i.e. that if a respondent revealed a fundamental attitude in his answer to any one of the questions, he was also likely to respond similarly to the remaining ones. The results are summarized below.

Instrumental attitudes seem to be gaining a wider acceptance— probably at the cost of fundamental attitudes. This is particularly true of the younger generation. A statistically significant tendency to hold an instrumental orientation was noticed among the following categories of respondents: men, younger people, less educated people, divorced persons, unskilled workers, poorly adjusted individuals, those manifesting symptoms of insecurity. Fundamental attitudes were more strongly revealed in the following groups: women, older people, better educated people, unmarried or married but not divorced individuals, white collar workers, individuals without feelings of insecurity.

It should be noted that these two sets of attitudes were obviously relevant to the main subject of our investigation. Thus fundamentally-minded persons strongly condemned, both from the legal and moral point of view, various situations which were examples of the breaking of the norms regulating social interaction. Such persons were also more punitive in their attitudes, more likely to accept the law as such and more likely to cherish egalitarian principles. On the other hand, instrumentally minded persons tended to take the opposite position.

It would seem that these findings are important both for theory and for actual 'social engineering'. They give us a clearer view of the distribution of attitudes and inclinations towards moral and legal norms as well as recognizing the negative responses to them. Besides, the results provide an opportunity to determine generally adequate working strategies: the instrumentalist can be appealed to less efficiently by moral or ideological arguments, but he will be more responsive to businesslike considerations. However, persons with fundamentalist attitudes will be more vulnerable to moral appeals.

Another basic problem analysed in our study was the phenomenon of legal punitiveness as opposed to legal tolerance. The problem was especially interesting because our earlier study on the prestige of law had yielded data which seemed to be incompatible with similar Scandinavian results. The Polish research revealed that greater punitiveness was related to a lower social situation and poor psychological adjustment, while the Scandinavian studies found that it was related to higher levels of education. In Kutchinsky's summary of the Scandinavian research it is stated that:

'the general finding (concerning punitiveness in the Scandinavian studies) is that the more educated an individual is, the stronger is his tendency to be intolerant towards criminal behaviour. ... My former interpretation was that if an individual is more educated, he can be expected to identify himself more strongly with punitive agency, and less with the criminal. ... As can be seen from OBOP investigations discussed above, the prevailing tendency in Poland is a completely opposite one, i.e. the more educated an individual is the greater likelihood there is that he will be tolerant towards unlawful behaviour. The question is should the Scandinavian and Polish results be considered as pointing to a dynamic interaction between the socio-economic and cultural systems on the one hand, and the valid systems of law on the other. Briefly and in rather simplified terms the position may be as follows: it is possible that the differences between the Scandinavian countries and Poland are related to the diversity of their socio-economic, cultural or legal systems. With this approach, Polish society might appear as more progressive than the Scandinavian, or the cause of the differences may be traced to the characteristics of the two types of legal system; or perhaps the Polish legal system is more rigoristic than the Scandinavian judicial patterns. Or else, perhaps both factors are working together. At any rate the latter factor is easier to identify empirically.'[9]

However if we take a closer look at the results we find that the suggested explanations of the differences are not satisfactory. We must assume that there are different types of punitiveness and tolerance and each of these types can appear with various intensities in different social systems. In general, punitiveness can be defined either as a greater severity than average in a given environment or social system, or else as a tendency to select more severe punishments from among those which are available. By tolerance can be meant, respectively, a leniency beyond that which is usual within a given environment or social system or else a tendency to select the most mild punishment out of those which can be applied, or even to reject punishment altogether. It should be noted (as is revealed by a comparison of earlier data with the present) that various types of punitiveness and tolerance can be found in many fields of social life. It can be assumed that there are many varieties of punitiveness and tolerance, such as those concerning matters of discipline, those concerning the uses that can be made of title to property, those concerning abuses against elementary forms of social interaction, and finally, 'pure' punitiveness and 'pure' tolerance.

Leaving aside for the moment the problem of the discrepancies between the Polish and Scandinavian studies, we shall now present some results relating to the social determinants of various types of the two attitudes discussed.

In fact it turned out that there are actually various types of punitiveness and tolerance and that they are empirically related in different ways with other social variables. Thus the following classes of respondents were more punitive than others on disciplinary issues involving a thorough punctual and proper respect for minor administrative regulations: more educated persons, those in jobs or professions enjoying a relatively high prestige, individuals without symptoms of feelings of insecurity, the 'fundamentalists', and those positively adjusted to their environment.

It is also interesting to compare the data on tolerance and punitiveness on disciplinary issues as yielded by the general population survey with materials from the research on particular groups (judges and recidivists). Thus, the judges are always more punitive in such matters than the general population, while the recidivists are always much more tolerant of disciplinary infractions than the average law-abiding citizen.

Data on tolerance of and punitiveness towards abuses concerning title to property reveal similar relationships as in the case of disciplinary issues. Thus, the following categories of respondent reacted more punitively towards abuses related to property: the better educated, those with higher occupational status, persons without feelings of insecurity, the 'fundamentalists', and well adjusted individuals.

Again a comparison of the responses of the general population sample with those of the special groups is instructive. What is revealed is a lack of essential differences in condemnations declared by various groups of respondents; all the apparent differences can be accounted for by differing levels of education.

Punitiveness and tolerance towards basic breaches of elementary norms of social interaction reveal somewhat different distinctions than do the cases discussed above. (These attitudes were found in an evaluation of moral or legal opinion of behaviour such as: refusing to help a person whose life is in danger when help could be given; an attempt to commit suicide; polygamy; addiction to alcohol; marital unfaithfulness.) Thus, the following categories of persons were more punitive in their condemnation: elderly people; widowed persons; better educated persons; workers; people with working class backgrounds; the 'fundamentalists'; those without symptoms of feelings of insecurity.

'Pure' punitiveness and tolerance appear to be determined by factors similar to those identified in the investigations on the prestige of law. Thus, poorer social background and impaired psychological adjustment is related to a greater punitiveness of the 'pure' type, while 'pure' tolerance is related to positive social and psychological situations.

These results suggest a number of important consequences. Firstly, the inconsistency between the Scandinavian and Polish data seems to be resolved: it may perhaps be that in both the jurisdictions studied 'pure' punitiveness is greatest among the less educated groups, but that better educated groups are also punitive towards breaches against discipline and order, against property rights and against elementary norms of interaction. Secondly, the fundamental attitude is correlated with different types of punitiveness thus providing a measure to determine the degree of internalization of norms in the processes of socialization. Indeed, if the fundamental attitude is considered to be a result of the internalization of a norm, or of an acceptance of it as one's own, we can say that the norm has become an element of the fundamental attitude. But then this attitude can be considered as a characteristic symptom and a measure of the progress of socialization in the given period. Thirdly, it turns out that there are significant and not surprising differences between the type of punitiveness or tolerance in various types of sub-cultures. The judges respect disciplinary regulations to a far greater degree, and react much more strongly against breaches than the average population, the latter being in turn much more punitive in this respect than the recidivists.

The programme of studies on legal and moral attitudes also included an analysis of what might be called individually and socially oriented ethics. By individually oriented ethics we mean a set of regulative norms governing behaviour towards other members of small, formal or informal groups. Thus, in general, individual ethics condemn theft, murder, adultery, fraud and false witness—or in other words, actions which may harm others in 'face to face' relationships. Whilst such forms of deviant behaviour have not necessarily been experienced by group members, abhorrence of them is a part of the common consciousness. Consequently, underlying the norms of individualistic ethics are various elementary types of behaviour approved of or condemned in face to face human contacts.

On the other hand, the norms of socially oriented ethics refer to the social roles and positions which are, or can be, occupied by an individual. The predominating aspect of such ethics is that there is no evaluation of the individual's personal qualities or of his conduct as a person, but rather of the effect caused by his occupation of a definite position in the social structure.

Our general conclusion is that the traditional model of individualistic ethics is the prevailing one. However, in the context of some kinds of behaviour, and particularly of economic behaviour, social ethics are more important.

As is shown by the data, two categories of respondents are socially oriented in their ethical attitudes. The first includes those who have a negative appreciation of social matters within their experience and who consequently more or less consciously desire social change. It may be supposed, then, that persons who demand changes represent the vested interests of their reference groups. Indeed some elements of such a relationship have been recorded. The fact that some symptoms of a social orientation on issues concerning economic affairs were emphasized by respondents in the lowest educational group, by those with peasant backgrounds and by skilled workers—and by no other respondents—seems to confirm this idea. The other category of respondents who had been expected to reveal a social orientation in ethics were persons with highly developed social involvement, i.e. those whose range of concerns extended beyond their immediate individual and family interests. We believed that they would identify themselves with broader problems and with social strata or classes, sometimes as champions of their original group, and sometimes representing the interests opposed to those of the groups to which they belonged. Although no such relationships can be directly deduced from the data, this may be because our research techniques were not sufficiently sophisticated to discover such relationships.

However, the available data on individual ethical orientation indirectly supports the above hypothesis. As we know from other sources, there is a certain type of personality in which individual interests are predominant, its main characteristics being: feelings of insecurity, instrumental attitudes, poor social adjustment, employment as self-employed craftsmen, higher education and home centred orientation. But these are precisely the characteristics which, as we have said, favour an individualistic orientation in ethics.

The next problem investigated was the postulated penal responsibility for offences committed in the course of helping a family member or a stranger in difficulties. Though this might seem a minor issue, one of the researchers, Maria Łoś, came to some interesting conclusions. There were respondents who revealed an egalitarian attitude (i.e. they were apt to treat equally the offences motivated by family solidarity and 'altruistic' ones motivated by a disinterested desire to help others), and on the other hand there were family oriented respondents who belonged to the following categories: 'they were people with strong feelings of insecurity, convinced that others are against them, poorly adjusted to life, in bad material conditions, uneducated and trained in poorly rewarded skills; in short, they were persons who could expect with a greater probability than others that they would suffer hardships together with families, while some psychological predisposition or unfortunate experience inclined them to see others as hostile or indifferent towards them. The percentage of socially involved people and of members of organizations is relatively low, so that

88

they are frequently lonely and passive people who do not expect help from any organization. Considering the low social status of their parents, we can suppose that many of them have known poverty in childhood. Besides, it should be emphasized that they are usually persons responsible for supporting their families, and thus married persons, the aged and the widowed are over-represented compared with the unmarried or divorced. Remarkable also is the relatively high percentage of persons of practising religious persuasion'.[10]

The above results might be somewhat unreliable since some of the investigated issues might seem abstract and rather detached from everyday experience. To establish the degree of reliability of the answers (i.e. their eventual consistency or inconsistency with the actual behaviour of respondents), a supplementary study was included in the research.

A comparison of the answers given with actual behaviour was attempted. The idea, contributed by J. Kwaśniewski, was to ask the respondents (city dwellers only) how frequently, if at all, they crossed the street when the red beacon is on, provided that it is quite safe, i.e. no car is approaching (in principle this is forbidden by the Polish traffic regulations). The respondents were also asked to justify their behaviour. An analysis of these responses was supplemented by observation of the behaviour of people in similar situations. The number of people who do, or do not, cross the street was counted. The observed persons were not those who were asked to describe their behaviour but, as those groups were large, we could reasonably expect that they were comparable. Remarkably it turned out that the distribution of verbal declarations and of the observed behaviour was quite consistent. This finding (similarly to some other detailed results, such as declarations of instrumental attitudes by divorced persons, as one would expect in those who had broken the basic marital norm) seems to support the consistency of the research data with actual behaviour. Indeed for a further verification of the survey data, intensive interviews with 38 persons (20 women and 18 men) were carried out. An analysis of the interviews showed that they were essentially parallel with the results of the national survey.

'An analysis of the materials collected seems to confirm once again the usefulness of open-ended interviews to increase the interpretative sensitivity of statistical results collected by a questionnaire. The results collected by means of each of the two methods are mutually consistent, and the extensive material of the interviews allows us to gain a better insight into the mechanism of attitude formation revealed by the questionnaire. Such a double procedure seems to be particularly advisable when studying such complex problems as legal and moral attitudes.'[11]

COMPARATIVE INVESTIGATIONS ON LEGAL AND MORAL ATTITUDES IN DIFFERENT SOCIAL SYSTEMS

Historians and economists have already discussed the diversity of the social determinants of various legal systems. It has become obvious that such systems are very heterogeneous and that their character is related to the social structures within which they operate. It is therefore unlikely that legal precepts or institutions of one system could be compared with those belonging to a different system, without taking into account their particular social, economic and political contexts and their divergent roles.

Theoretical discussions of the nature of the state and law are already well developed. However, even if we ignore the fact that anthropological findings have been neglected, it still remains true that the comparative analysis of legal norms has constituted almost the sole type of theoretical considerations. Whenever the historical or economic methods are abandoned the use of unsystematic impressions tends to take their place.

We therefore turn to an examination of the complex investigations which we designed to compare various attitudes towards similar legal and moral issues in different societies. The main intention of the project was to test the utility of certain intra-systematic research techniques and to build up a systematic basis for further empirically testable macro-systemic studies. Our interpretation of the results is of a tenative nature, but we have attempted to limit our conclusions to matters which are given a fair degree of support by the existing data. Our conclusions are however of two different kinds: those drawn from the data actually available and working hypotheses for further investigations. As far as the latter are concerned our study can be considered as a pilot enquiry.

Earlier enquiries had stimulated the 1966 Polish survey on legal and moral sentiments. These were carried out in Sweden in 1947, Denmark in 1954 and 1962, Norway in 1961 and 1962—all these studies are summarized by B. Kutchinsky in his article 'Law and Education' (*Acta Sociologica* 1966, Vol. 10) and the Finnish investigation is summarized by K. Mäkelä in his article 'Public Sense of Justice and Judicial Practice' (*Acta Sociologica* 1966, Vol. 10). It should also be noted that the Polish 1966 survey stimulated similar ventures in the Netherlands, Belgium and Brazil. The Dutch investigation, the most elaborate of all these later endeavours, has mainly been concerned with issues of tax regulation,[12] but it also dealt with some problems central to the Polish research. The Belgian study (carried out by J. Van Houtte) is reported on in this volume. The Brazilian research[13] is still in the planning stages and its design is likely to be modified according to the Polish and Dutch experience.

The common feature of all these ventures is that they are focused mainly on what is usually called 'legal sentiment', i.e. on opinions about and attitudes towards legal and moral norms functioning in various social systems. The fact that recent research—in particular the Scandinavian and Polish studies on the prestige of law—are closely related, means that the approach is one of a 'cooperative comparative study'. Independent studies on similar problems are undertaken in various countries, with due consideration for the specific structural, economic, legal and political peculiarities of each country. Such programmes have a number of advantages: they offer diagnostic knowledge about several societies; they facilitate comparisons of selected aspects of the investigated populations; they allow emphasis on peculiar and specific problems; they highlight the central hypotheses which may then be empirically tested; and they provide an analytic basis for subsequent cross-cultural designs.

Some of the results which are available in the present phase of the research work are described below. However before we turn to them in detail, we must digress somewhat and discuss some notions concerning comparative studies in general and comparative studies of legal systems in particular.

What we call 'cooperative' investigations may be opposed to what may be defined as the '*a priori*-centralistic' approach. Within the latter approach, some preconceived research conception is

91

taken for granted. On the basis of existing knowledge, various societies are selected for comparative analysis and detailed hypotheses to be tested in those systems are derived from the *a prioric* general theories. It should be pointed out at the outset that this kind of approach involves a high risk of failure, since it may well turn out in the course of the research that the social systems under investigation cannot be compared at all in terms of the generally accepted hypotheses. In addition, factors left out of the initial research strategy may turn out to be significant, while the existing working assumptions make it impossible to grasp them with sufficient precision. Or again, various obstacles which had seemed to be of an administrative character may turn out to be methodological problems which prove difficult to solve. Worst of all, results of the studies based on *a priori* assumptions may perforce be so vague and so uninteresting that comparative analysis of different societies is precluded.

These methodological difficulties are further increased by other significant considerations. In the recently developing methodology of comparative investigation there is not sufficient clarity as to whether such studies may be applied to social systems as defined by nations, states or social-political belief. Besides, various comparisons between social systems can be carried out at sub-system level. Thus, for example, studies of the functioning of various legal systems could be compared with data on several sub-cultures within a given society which tend to support or oppose the legally relevant principles. There are still further methodological difficulties involved in comparative investigation. For in such investigations of various societies the factors selected as the dependent variables can be either homogeneous or not. A legal system is a homogeneous or uniform variable because it is always a uniform and adequate formal system produced by a society. Similarly, different social settings (such as nations) evolve their peculiar national characters which are unique syntheses of various historically determined political, social and economic factors.

Comparative studies concerning such problems as the family, work, local authorities, leisure, etc. are in a methodologically less advantageous position than studies of law. For example, in different social systems the model of the family can be shaped in various ways, not only as a result of differences in the political systems in which the family may function, but also as a result of other influences, such as the prevailing economic, social and demographic conditions along with their peculiar modifying combinations. Thus in these cases we have a greater variety of independent variables influencing the dependent ones. In this connection, diagnostic and theoretical comparative investigations must be distinguished. A diagnostic study can explore the diversity or similarity of some characteristics, such as family models, leisure habits, or the functioning of the local authorities in various societies. However nothing more than that is possible. It can only be stated that in a given social system there are monogamous families, or that nuclear family units prevail, while in another society there are polygamous or extended families. Theoretical comparative studies differ from the diagnostic type in that they attempt, besides fact finding, to verify definite relationships. As has already been mentioned, verification of theoretical relationships at various levels is only possible when the variables studied are uniform in character. Since the legal systems and their elements are marked by the uniformity required for comparative analysis, analytic comparisons of legal systems are particularly valuable, since they can provide not only diagnostic data, but also form a basis for formulating adequate hypotheses concerning more general regularities. However, the *a priori*-centralistic approach to comparative analyses of legal systems still suffers from some limitations, in spite of the broader opportunities which are opened up by the comparative method. illustrative of such setbacks is the comparative work of W. Evan on non-socialist legal systems.[14] Two types of data were juxtaposed: various features of social systems such as urbanization, industrialization, religion, level of economic development, etc., on the one hand, and data concerning the function of the investigated legal system on the other. Here are some of the results: (a) there is a positive correlation between the level of bureaucratization, industrialization, urbanization, professionalism and the number of lawyers employed in the society; (b) there is a positive correlation between the growth of bureaucracy and the number of law faculties in that society's universities; (c) there is a positive relationship between the number of law faculties and the number of those who participate in legislative activities; (d) the role of the police can be conceived in two ways: either as an institution whose major task is to maintain and support the legal order, or as an agency of political patronage. If we accept this distinction we can see that

93

the role of guarding the legal order is related (in terms of the data used in the study) with high levels of industrialization, urbanization, education and professionalism. The role of political patronage is connected, respectively, with low levels of industrialization, urbanization, education and professionalization.

The results of studies of this type are rather vague. Several of their basic concepts, like 'persons engaged in legislative activities' or 'political patronage' do not mean the same thing in different social systems. Hence it is doubtful whether the basic characteristics—which anyway are ambiguous in their meaning—can be reasonably compared at all. The type of investigation which we have called 'cooperative' tries to avoid these disadvantages of the *a priori*-centralistic approach.

Cooperative investigations make use of the results of existing investigations, treating them as pilot sudies. This is done in two phases. During the first phase there is analysis of the legal constructs that are peculiar to the investigated social systems and an identification of those which constitute a common denominator. In this phase the following problems are the main focus: analysis of cases of similar functioning of different legal constructs within similar social systems; and analysis of eventual cases of similar functioning of different legal constructs in different social systems. The experience built up during this first phase of cooperative investigation is indispensible for a common, synthetic reasearch tool (a questionnaire), for clarifying basic concepts, and for preparing comparable statistical procedures and techniques of data coding etc., thus forming a starting point for the second phase. This second phase may be devoted to a more systematic study of legal systems, accounting for their peculiarities (determined by tradition), similarities (as, for example, between the legal systems of socialist countries), and the eventual identification of shared legal constructs or basic norms in different social settings. We can hazard a guess that there are no such constructs, except for issues of minor social importance, like incest, though a tendency towards a greater global uniformity is remarkable, as is illustrated by the Charter of Human Rights.

The Polish, Dutch, Belgian and Brazilian surveys ought to be considered as an attempt at international cooperation in collecting experience for the first phase. We shall discuss some of the results, with some reference to earlier endeavours treated as pilot studies.

94

The research has been devoted to studying the legal sentiments prevailing within various social systems, and consequently is based mainly on analysis of verbal declaration. In this context the recurrent problem of the relationship between declared opinion and actual behaviour arises once more. A pertinent and simple model of the complex relationship has been suggested by Z. Sufin: 'It turned out that [the declared attitudes and behavioural stances] towards some values have been consistent, while towards others they have not. A number of explanatory hypotheses were tested, leading to a general model of interpretation.

The General Model of Evaluation

The postulated ---------------------------------- The realization
values . . . of a value

.   .   .

.   .   .

.   .   .

.   .   .

Declarative   Acceptance The need of
acknowledge-   realization
ment

The model is based on the assumption that there are three distinct types of link between the postulating of a value and its realization. The attitude towards the value can be marked by various degrees of involvement, expressed by a mere verbal acknowledgement, an acceptance (internalization), or a need of realization of the value ... caused by external conditions'.[15]

As has been mentioned, this kind of difficulty can be overcome by various methods. For example topical problems can be selected which are likely to be emotionally highly significant for the respondents, thus inducing them to express their real views: this is more likely to occur if the issues tackled in the question are less relevant to a respondent's personal situation. Special experiments can be designed in which the declared attitudes, e.g. of punitiveness versus tolerance, are compared with the actual behaviour corresponding to the declarations.[16] Yet another strategy

95

employed in the comparative investigations discussed, consists in introducing special populations whose members hold particular attitudes systematically and continuously biased by their broader life situation. Thus, besides the general population samples supplementary control populations were introduced. As we have remarked earlier, in the Polish survey such populations were judges and recidivists, and in the Dutch research the respective groups were tax officers and recidivists. Though these methodological devices do not totally control for discrepancies between declared opinions or judgements and those which form the actual bases for behaviour, nevertheless such techniques allow us to assess with reasonable reliability the differences between the two.

The comparative studies of various social systems, supplemented with sub-system enquiries (studies of sub-cultures, specific populations, etc.) make possible the following tentative observations: (a) when the breaking of basic norms of social interaction is involved, people in general tend to condemn more strongly and to demand more severe legal sanctions than legal officers. Thus judges in Poland and in Finland and tax officers in Holland are inclined to be somewhat more lenient towards breaches of elementary principles of social interaction than the general population. This interesting finding is explained not by the fact that legal officers are less exacting but by the fact that they are more aware of the inadequacies of punishment as a tool of social engineering and they are in a position to assess more precisely the effect of more severe penal sanctions. (b) The general population condemns breaches of basic norms of social interaction only slightly more strongly than those who break the law themselves. Both the Polish and Dutch data revealed that basic social values are fairly strongly internalized by the whole population, and that those who break the law differ only slightly as to the intensity of their moral indignation about the breaking of generally accepted rules. Supplementary studies of various legal sub-cultures and in particular of negatively correlated ones such as full-time sub-cultures of delinquency would probably show that for such people there is a drastic lowering of the intensity of moral condemnation. However, even if such studies are still lacking, we can refer to the investigations of the recidivist sub-population to modify the proposition along the following lines: the slight lowering of moral indignation is related to a very significant lowering of the demand for legal sanction.[17] Thus, whenever moral condemnation falls slightly, legal condemnation declines much more. This proposition seems to shed important light on the moral origin of legal condemnation and draws our attention to the store of moral values which, whilst they may seem to be irrelevant to law, are apt to hinder or support the functioning of law to a significant extent. (c) In questions of procedure and order legal officers always condemn more strongly cases of misbehaviour than do the general population which, in its turn, always condemns more strongly than those who break the law. The Polish and Dutch general population are both marked by fairly strong negative attitudes towards the breaking of principles of legal order. Significantly, however, in both countries the legal officers, probably because of the nature of their profession, always condemn more strongly this kind of misbehaviour, while recidivists, as if because of the nature of their 'trade', always have less respect for such norms. (d) A legal condemnation induces also a moral one. Before we started the Polish survey we had supposed that there were various types of behaviour regulated by administrative and technical prescriptions which were morally indifferent, i.e. it was supposed that the breaking of such prescriptions would not lead to moral condemnation. Surprisingly it turned out in the Polish research and this was confirmed by the Dutch data, that legal condemnation (the inclusion of behaviour into the class of legally prescribed behaviour) is related to a tendency to cover the given behaviour by moral judgement as well. It is remarkable that this relationship has also been confirmed by sub-system enquiries. Thus the Polish study on recidivists revealed that they, like the general sample, tended to condemn morally the behaviours, which in their opinion, should be condemned by law. (e) A high level of moral indignation together with its formalization in regulations of the penal law brings about the demand for legal sanctions; a high level of moral indignation which is not formally confirmed by law, does not bring about such a demand. This proposition results from a comparison of the Polish and Dutch data on attitudes toward adultery. It is strongly condemned in both countries (70.3% of the Polish sample and 81.8% of the Dutch general sample strongly condemned adultery). However in the Netherlands the prevalent sentiment is formalized and adultery is a crime (though the relevent section of the penal code is 'dead' and no longer applied in practice). In Poland there is no law against adultery.

97

As a consequence 53·3% of the Dutch sample and only 16·7% of the Polish sample demanded penal sanctions for adultery. (f) Whether penal measures are seen as aimed at reformation, rather than punishment is highly correlated with level of education. Comparative data from the Polish investigation and the Norwegian ones (in this context considered as pilot studies) confirm this relationship. The quoted findings (mainly diagnostic in character) have been confirmed for various societies. However not all of the tested hypotheses have been confirmed by the data. For example the Polish data gave no confirmation for the proposition, supported by Norwegian results, that women tend to be more severe than men in their moral condemnation (except women who are big city dwellers and those who are materially well off), while men tend to be more censorious about property crimes. (g) Pure punitiveness is inversely related to level of education. Punitive attitudes about the breaking of the basic norms of social interaction, about breaches of minor regulations and about depredations against property are more marked in better educated respondents, while the respective tolerant attitudes decrease correspondingly.

It can be seen from the above results that some propositions find supplementary support in the systematic-comparative analyses, while others do not or are modified. However the comparative studies of the cooperative type provide interesting information of still another character. Thus, for example, it was found in an introductory investigation prior to the proper survey that certain moral and legal attitudes typical for Polish society had not appeared to a significant degree in Holland. For example the social orientation in ethics (the tendency to appreciate an individual with reference to the social consequences of his role-performing or his social position, rather than because of his personal qualities) has been marked among the Polish population but hardly so in the investigated area among the Dutch. So among Poles negative appreciation of the social consequences of the fact that somebody used to be a Nazi generally take an upper hand over his purely personal merits. In Dutch evaluations, private qualities would determine the overall balance. Similarly, Poles believe that for social reasons cultural relics in the possession of private persons should be protected against an unlimited right to dispose of private property. The Dutch declared a primacy of the right of an individual to dispose of his property at will.

In sum, cooperative investigations allow us to grasp more systematically, and with greater precision, the peculiarities of various social systems and of the legal systems functioning within them. They generate, and at the same time satisfy a need for a more comprehensive theory of sociology of law.

NOTES

1. A. Turska, *Póczucie prawne a świadomośe prawa*; 'Państwo i prawo' 1961, No. 2, p. 243.
2. J. Gohen, R. A. Robson, A. Bates, *Parental Authority*; Rutgers University Press, 1958. This study should be regarded as a pattern for subsequent enquiries of this type.
3. F. C. Newman, S. S. Surrey, *Legislation—Causes and Materials*, New York 1950; St Ehrlich, Grupy nacisku, Warszawa 1962.
4. B. Russell, *Power*, London 1948.
5. A. Podgorecki, *Zjawiska prawne w opinni publicznej*, Warszawa 1964, the chapter on parental authority ('Wladza rodzicielska').
6. A. Iwańska-Wagner, *Good Fortune*, Washington 1956.
7. A. Podgorecki, *Prestiz prawa*, Warszawa 1966.
8. The survey on the legal and moral attitudes of the Polish society was carried out by the Ośrodek Badania Opinii Publicznej. The questionnaire was designed by: A. Podgorecki, J. Kurczewski, J. Kwaśniewski, M. Łoś. The main study had been preceded by two pilot probes (one of them expanded into the analytic interview elaborated as a separate study); it was carried out in December 1966. Both the urban and rural populations were studied. 3167 repondents, i.e. 95.9% of the initial sample of 3312 persons were actually interviewed. A general report of the study was published in the book *Poglady spoleczenstwa polskiego na moralnośc i prawo*, Warszawa 1971.
9. B. Kutchinsky, 'Law and Education', Evian 1966, the VIth World Congress of Sociology, a typescript. Later works of B. Kutchinsky bring a lot of new interesting results in this area.
10. M. Łoś Opinia publiczna o przestępstwach nieegoistycznylch, in: *Poglady spoleczeństawa polskiego na moralnośc i prawo*, op. cit., pp. 150 177.
11. J. Kobel, 'Poczucie prawne i moralne' (an unpublished B.A. dissertation), Social Sciences Faculty, Warsaw University 1968.
12. Initial results of those investigations have been reported in an unpublished paper by P. Vinke (Netherlands), 'Internal Acceptation of the Legal Rules. A Law-sociological Research'.
13. The design has been undertaken by Prof. A. de Miranda Rosa of the Gama Filho University, Rio de Janeiro, Brasil.
14. W. M. Evans, 'Toward a data Archive of Legal Systems: An Exploratory Cross-National Analysis' (unpublished data presented during the VIth International Congress of Sociology, Evian 1966.)
15. Z. Sufin, *Kultura pracy*, Warszawa 1968, p. 172.

16. Research by J. Kurczewski, 'Struktura pogledów no prawo i ich powiazania wewnetrzne' (an unpublished B.A. dissertation), Social Science Faculty, Warsaw University 1966.
17. This proposition was additionally verified by data from the research by A. Kojder, 'Prawne i moralne postawy wienźniów-recydywistów' (an unpublished B.A. dissertation), Social Sciences Faculty, Warsaw University.

'THE LEGAL CONSCIOUSNESS': A SURVEY OF RESEARCH ON KNOWLEDGE AND OPINION ABOUT LAW

Berl Kutchinsky

From time to time the concept of 'the public sense of justice' or 'the legal consciousness of the common man' appears in discussion of legal issues, be it in Parliamentary debates, in everyday arguments, in newspaper columns or in textbooks on legal philosophy. It is a strange and mythical concept which has a variety of roles in social life attributed to it: sometimes it is considered a strong and active force, setting limits to or putting demands on legislators as well as the courts of justice; sometimes it is considered rather a weak and passive mechanism which can be shaped and moulded by politicians, law enforcement authorities, and educators through the threat of punishment or through good example. A 'strong legal consciousness' is sometimes considered the *cause* of adherence to law (sometimes it is just another word for that) while a 'weak legal consciousness' is considered the cause of crime and evil.

Until recently almost anything could be said about the shape and content of the 'general sense of justice', since nobody really knew what it was. This is no longer the case. During recent years there has been a rapidly growing interest in this phenomenon among social scientists. The study of public knowledge and attitudes regarding law, crimes, legal institutions and related issues (KOL[1]) has become a major field of research within the sociology of law; scores of empirical investigations of this kind have been carried out, and even more are in the making.

The purpose of this article[2] is to present some of the major topics and findings in this area of research. It is in some ways an attempt to see what is fact and what is fantasy in the idea of the 'general sense of justice'.

Law, legal consciousness, and legal behaviour

Let us first look at some of the assumptions underlying some traditional as well as some modern theories on the functioning of law in society, and let us see what evidence studies on KOL bring to bear on these assumptions.

It is a traditional juridical viewpoint that the legal rules (*Leges* and other legal sources) of a nation define in an unambiguous way which acts are forbidden and which are permitted for the citizens of that nation. The juridical tradition also takes for granted that these legal rules are adhered to by the vast majority of citizens. This agreement between legal rules and legal behaviour, which has been called the 'co-variance theory' (Aubert, 1954) is more or less accepted as a fact not only by legislators but also by most legal philosophers and sociologists. There has of course been some dispute about the causality of this hypothesized co-variance. It is generally agreed that the reason most people do not commit murders or other serious crimes is not that these acts are forbidden in the penal law, but rather that they are morally condemned. It is also generally accepted that with regard to these classical crimes, morality preceded the law and not vice versa. There is serious argument, however, as to whether the existence of the laws and the threat of punishment are necessary to *uphold* moral attitudes—will morality decay sooner or later if it is not supported by official laws?

Quite a different discussion has taken place concerning *new laws*. While the legislators traditionally seem to expect as a matter of course that the mere passage of a bill in Parliament will automatically affect the relevant behaviour of the citizen, some legal philosophers and sociologists (among others Savigny, 1814; Sumner, 1906; Ehrlich, 1913), at least in theory, took the opposite standpoint. They maintained that any law, including new law, was only 'effective' to the extent that it coincided with the *Volksgeist*, the *Volkways*, the *Rechtsbewusstsein* (legal consciousness). Today, all scholars agree that law can indeed affect behaviour—the empirical evidence is too conspicuous to permit a contrary view. There is a certain amount of disagreement, however, as to how this effect is brought about. The older viewpoint, namely that law becomes effective due to the deterrent threat of punishment is no longer adhered to as the only principle. Instead, or in addition, a variety of
102

theories have been put forward, sometimes expressed in philosophical language using words like 'moral', 'conscience', 'sense of duty' or 'social habits', sometimes expressed in the jargon of modern psychology and sociology as 'internalized norms', 'formation of attitudes' or 'belief systems'. These theories, however, all have one thing in common: they postulate some sort of a mediator between law and behaviour, which we have called legal consciousness. This construct, having both cognitive and emotive aspects, is sometimes (for instance by Podgorecki) regarded as an 'intervening variable' in the sense that it intervenes causally between the two otherwise unrelated variables, the law and the behaviour. Sometimes it is rather a hypothetical construct which can be part of a complicated model of interaction (e.g. Stjernquist, 1963).

In any case, whether we are dealing with old laws or new ones, it would seem relevant to study the appropriate public conceptions of these laws, including the possible formation of moral attitudes. In what follows, we shall deal with some of the explicit or implicit assumptions concerning the various relationships between law, legal knowledge, legal attitudes, and legal behaviour.

Knowledge about law

Traditional legislative procedure is based on the unquestioned assumptions that once a bill has been passed in Parliament and duly published, the necessary knowledge about the new law is automatically disseminated among the public. Empirical evidence (and common sense as well) shows that this assumption is wrong. Just to mention one example: in a survey of the knowledge about the Suicide Act of 1961 possessed by average Englishmen, Walker & Argyle (1964) found only 16% who knew that attempted suicide was no longer a crime. No less than 75% thought that attempted suicide was criminal, although the repeal had taken place only a year before the survey.

The fact that the general public has little knowledge about some specific laws is not very surprising. More unexpected perhaps are the findings that quite often knowledge about *specific laws* is rather poor in those *specific groups* for which the laws were made.

103

Thus, Aubert, Eckhoff & Sveri (1952) in their famous study of the *Norwegian Housemaid* Law (regulating working conditions for housemaids) found very low awareness[3] of the existence of the Housemaid Law and, accordingly, very little knowledge about its contents among the housemaid and their employers, the housewives. Only 10% of the housemaid and 17% of the housewives mentioned the law (which had only recently been passed) in connection with a series of questions designed to assess awareness of the law. Similar results appeared in another classic within the sociology of law, the study on *Working Hours and Holiday for Agricultural Workers* by Schmidt, Grantze & Roos (1946). As an answer to the question: 'Do you know what may happen, if you do not comply with the requirements of the law on working hours?', 33% of the employers and only 11% of the employees knew the correct answer (namely that they would be punished by a fine) (p. 770).

The results from these studies can hardly be generalized to apply to the knowledge of law in all types of special groups. Members of many special groups, such as business men, are forced to have very detailed knowledge about laws that regulate their behaviour (e.g. Aubert, 1950). The two studies mentioned are rather typical examples, however, of the results of legislation which has 'latent functions'. Sometimes, the dysfunctions of laws or the lack of enforcement are merely due to the clumsiness of its administration, or lack of knowledge about elementary marketing techniques. Quite often, however, one cannot avoid the suspicion that poor legislation and poor marketing of new laws is a result of the legislators' own ambivalent attitude towards the law (see the discussion by Aubert, 1966).

These two studies had another important element in common: both illustrated instances of adherence to the law independent of knowledge about the law. In other words: *knowledge about law is neither a necessary nor a sufficient condition for conformity to the law*. We shall return to this question later.

Another fact revealed by studies on KOL is the rather low level of knowledge about issues on which the *general* public might be expected to be well-informed. Thus, in a survey of adult Copenhageners Kutchinsky (1968) found only 3% who gave the correct answer to the question: 'Who passes laws?' Even the partially correct answer that laws are passed by the 'Folketing' was only given by a rather small number, 57% of the men and 22% of the women (Kutchinsky, 1968, p. 128f.). To a similar question: 'Who or what organ has charge of legislation in Hungary?' Kulcsár (1968) got 71% correct answers from the white-collar or professional respondents, while only 39% and 38% of city workers and the rural labourers, respectively, answered correctly (p. 53).

On the other hand, in the Danish investigation, there were 90% correct answers to the question: 'If you commit an offence without knowing that it is against the law, can you be punished for this?' (Kutchinsky, 1968, p. 129). And clearly, the knowledge of certain laws is widespread. Many sections of criminal law are in fact common knowledge, for instance laws prohibiting theft, murder and robbery. This does not affect the general conclusion, however that public knowledge concerning legal topics is considerably poorer than presumed by the legal authorities and by many scholars.

A few attempts to find a relationship between *criminal behaviour* and *poor knowledge about law* have shown that to the extent that these two factors are positively correlated, the correlation is probably due to common underlying factors. Kutchinsky (1968, p. 129) found that prisoners had a considerably poorer knowledge about law than men in the general population—even when social level was kept constant. However, the women had a similarly poor knowledge—without being criminal. Similarly, Syren & Thamm (1968) in a study on legal attitudes and self-reported crimes among school children found no *direct* relationship between the degree of knowledge about punitive reactions and the degree of self-reported criminality.

The relationship between specific *law-awareness and the corresponding legal and moral attitudes and behaviour,* is a question of special significance. Does awareness of the very fact that a certain type of behaviour is regulated by law influence attitudes and behaviour in relation to that law? More specifically: does 'criminalization' of a certain act create or increase (moral) condemnation of this act, while 'decriminalization' has the opposite effect?

Aubert *et al.* (1952) found no clear relationship between law-awareness and legal behaviour in relation to the new Housemaid Law (mentioned above). This may be due to the fact that the survey was carried out only one year after the enactment of the law and in consequence, very few housemaids or housewives knew

105

about the law. Indeed, a follow-up study six years later (Aubert, 1966) showed a 'highly significant relationship between the knowledge and behaviour among the housewives' (Aubert, 1966, p. 118). Aubert warns against considering this relationship as a causal one: both might be a function of a third independent variable. The nature of this independent variable which may have influenced both knowledge and behaviour is indicated by some data reported by the Housemaid Law Commission (*Instilling*, 1960, p. 47). When the respondents were asked where they had heard about the law, 75% of the housewives in the 1950 survey said they had heard about it on the radio or read about it in the newspapers or magazines, but only 12% had heard about the new law from associates (relatives, friends and so on). In 1956, only 50% of the housewives who knew about the law said they had obtained the information through the mass media, while the proportion who had been informed by associates had increased to 28%. (A similar, but not so significant shift had taken place among the housemaids.) These figures indicate that the positive correlation between legal knowledge and behaviour which had come about between 1950 and 1956 might be due to the increase in personal communications as against the impersonal mass media communications. A reasonable interpretation of this finding is that it was not the knowledge *per se* which brought about the changes in attitudes; rather, the increased knowledge was a by-product of a change in legal attitudes (increased *law acceptance*) as a consequence of peer influence. Similar conclusions could be made on the basis of an American study on public knowledge and attitudes towards chiseling (Smigel, 1953) and of a recent Dutch study of business men's knowledge about and attitudes towards Value Added Tax (Schuyt & Ruys, 1971).

A series of studies by Walker & Argyle (1964) and Berkowitz & Walker (1967) also concluded that peer influence was more important than the mere knowledge about law. These studies were directly designed to test one of the pre-suppositions behind the so called 'declaratory argument' often used by those who oppose liberalization of laws.[5] This argument asserts that 'whether a legal prohibition operates as a deterrent or not, to repeal it would give the impression that the conduct in question is no longer regarded by society as morally wrong' (Walker & Argyle, 1964, p. 570). Three studies were carried out in order to discover whether people's moral judgements were affected by their awareness as to the state

106

of the law.

The *first* study was a field-survey (briefly mentioned above) which took advantage of the fact that in 1961, the Suicide Act of the British Parliament provided that attempted suicide should no longer be a criminal offence. One year after the act came into force, 403 persons in different parts of Britain were interviewed concerning, among other things, knowledge about the Suicide Act and about legal and moral attitudes towards attempted suicide. Of those interviewed, only 16% knew that the law had been changed; 9% were unsure; the remainder believed that attempted suicide was still a criminal offence. Comparisons showed that there was 'no tendency for either men or women who knew of the change in the law to take a less strict moral view ... In other words, the figures failed to provide any support for the declaratory theory' (Walker & Argyle, 1964, p. 572).

The *second* study was an experiment in which 308 young men and women were asked to rate a number of acts (such as performing an abortion for different reasons, unintentional litter dropping, public drunkenness and use of obscene language in public) on a six-point scale, ranging from 'as wrong as possible' to 'very right'. The acts chosen were of such a kind that only very few people might be expected to know for certain whether they were prohibited by law or not. Half of the subjects were told that the acts to be rated were criminal offences, while the other half were told that they were not forbidden.

The results gave no support to the 'declaratory argument'. No significant differences appeared to occur between those who were told that a given type of conduct was a criminal offence and those who were told that it was not. On the contrary, there were a few cases in which the reference to the criminal law seemed to provoke an *antagonistic* reaction.

The authors were able to measure the effect of the 'majority view' on opinion and attitude change by giving the respondents fictitious results from a peer survey and noting the subsequent attitude change. They found that the effect which 'knowledge about law' failed to produce was easily accomplished by introducing the view of peers. By means of some additional items in the questionnaire, Walker and Argyle did, however, find some small but 'by no means negligible' minorities among the respondents who *said* that their moral attitudes towards a non-criminal activity, namely heavy

107

smoking, would become more censorious if Parliament passed a law making this form of behaviour a criminal offence.

These last mentioned findings, among other, inspired Berkowitz & Walker (1967) to conduct a *third* experiment. This time an attempt was made to *change* already expressed opinions about certain 'immoral acts'. Three groups completed questionnaires expressing degrees of (moral) condemnation of a number of acts. In a retest, using rating of the same acts, *one group* were told that recent changes in legislation had made some of the items 'legally permissible' while other items were now 'illegal'. A *second group* were told that 'over 80% of the students in a recent national survey strongly agreed with some of the statements and disagreed with some of the other statements'. The *third group* was a control group: like the other groups, they were told to 'think about the issue a bit more and perhaps alter the original judgements'.

Under these conditions, a small but nevertheless significant tendency was found for some people to let their attitudes be influenced by law awareness. The authors concluded, however, that 'knowledge of the existence of these laws ... does not have as much effect in changing the moral judgement as knowledge of a consensus of opinion among one's peers' (Berkowitz & Walker, p. 421).

Attitudes toward law and law-breaking

The attitudinal aspect of the 'legal consciousness' has often been investigated through studies of attitudes towards crimes. From the point of view of a co-variance theory two questions may be asked: Firstly, to what extent is the absolute fact of an act being forbidden by law accepted by the public? Secondly, to what extent does the seriousness of crimes in terms of the law (or court practice) coincide with the seriousness of these crimes in the view of the general population?

As far as the first of these questions is concerned, only a few studies have been carried out so far. Kutchinsky (1973) set out to measure what might be called 'the lower threshold' of the sex crime concept. In an interview survey, a representative sample of 398 adult men and women from Copenhagen were presented with

108

eight short descriptions of what the interviewer referred to as 'sexual acts'. In each case, the respondent was asked to say whether the act in question, according to his or her personal opinion, should be considered 'criminal' or not. Only one of the acts, a case of child molesting, was considered criminal by almost all the respondents (93% of both men and women). The remainder of the cases were considered criminal by 67% or less. One case, a woman being raped after having permitted petting, was considered criminal by only 12% of the respondents. In other words, there was substantial agreement that this latter act (which was definitely criminal according to the Penal Law) should not be considered criminal.

Similar discrepancies between what has been criminalized by the law and what the public considered to be criminal can undoubtedly be found in relation to other types of crime, such as crimes of property and violence. In some cases, the lack of co-variance is due to the law having become obsolete in relation to a liberalized public opinion. In other cases the discrepancy is merely due to the fact that the law does not operate with a lower limit of values: for instance, in connection with property, stealing a pennyworth of property is a crime, at least according to Danish criminal law. Thirdly, a discrepancy between the law and the public may be found in relation to relatively new laws, when the criminalization of certain types of conduct have not 'yet' managed to change public opinion (e.g. drunken driving). Finally, there are certain discrepancies which have probably always existed. Thus begging, although a crime in several countries, was probably never considered criminal by the public.

These general remarks about the lack of co-variance between law and public opinion as far as the absolute threshold of crime is concerned are also true, more or less, with regard to the relative *seriousness of crimes*. Public opinion about the seriousness of crimes has been the object of numerous studies, using a variety of meaurement techniques. Two of these studies, Rose & Prell (1955) and Makela (1966), directly compared the *public view* of the seriousness of crimes to that of the *criminal law* and *court practice*. Since these two studies, an American and a Finnish one, arrived at rather contradictory conclusions, we shall deal with them in some detail.

Rose & Prell (1955) conducted a pilot investigation in order to test the hypothesis that 'there is a significant discrepancy between three things: (1) the punishments specified in law for given crimes;

109

(2) the punishments actually meted out for these crimes; and (3) the popular judgement as to what punishments should be assigned to these crimes' (p. 248). This hypothesis was based on the general assumption that there would be a 'cultural lag' between the laws that were made centuries ago and the public conceptions which were expected to have undergone changes. In order to test their hypothesis, Rose & Prell chose thirteen offences, each of which might be considered 'minor felony' according to the California Penal Code. Each type of offence was transformed into a one sentence description to be rated by three groups of student subjects, using the method of paired comparisons. The results of these ratings were compared to the average punishments meted out to prisoners in a Californian prison.

Findings strongly supported the hypothesis. The authors concluded that 'there is no positive relation between the severity of punishments actually accorded to the prisoners . . . and the judgements we obtained concerning the seriousness of the crimes for which these criminals were punished' (Rose & Prell, 1955, p. 252f.). An interesting finding was that *child-beating* which had the lowest maximum penalty among the 13 selected felonies, was the type of crime considered *most* serious by the respondents.

There was also a lack of relationship between the punishments permitted by law and the actual punishments meted out to prisoners. As noticed by the authors, this may be simply an artefact of the limited list of crimes chosen to study, all of which had more or less the same 'penal law severity' in terms of minimum and maximum penalty.

While the study of Rose & Prell was a small pilot study with certain weaknesses inherent in the choice and number of subjects and in the method of comparing items (as pointed out by the authors themselves), a very comprehensive study has been carried out by Makela (1966) in Finland. Makela used eleven different crimes, each described in one or two sentences. This list of items was presented to a Gallup survey sample of over two thousand adult persons in Finland. In a face-to-face interview, they were asked with respect to each of the crimes, what kind of punishment they would consider appropriate. A card containing a range of alternative sentences was handed to the respondents; the range was from acquittal to 'unconditional imprisonment, over 1 year'. The choice of punishments could be fitted into a scale from 0–5, thus permitting various kinds of processing. In order to obtain comparable data of judicial practice, the same questionnaire was mailed to all judges in Finland's general courts of first instance. Questionnaires were returned from 143 judges—a response rate of about 65%. Finally, Makela obtained data on punishments actually meted out to persons who had been tried and convicted in a court of first instance for the same crime during the year 1960.

In view of the above findings of Rose & Prell (1955) some of Makela's findings were quite spectacular. Thus, a correlation of no less than 0·96 was found between the mean penalties demanded by the public and by the judges, i.e. there was almost total agreement.[6] Similarly high correlations were found[7] between the rank orders of the seriousness of crimes according to the *law* (based on maximum penalty prescribed), *judicial practice* (based on the mean length of sentence), *judges' survey* (based on mean length of sentence), and the *public survey* (based on mean choice of punitive category). When one type of crime (obviously atypically serious) was excluded, extremely high rank order correlations were obtained (ranging between 0·92 and 0·98).

These results point clearly to the fact that in the Finnish study as opposed to the American one there was an almost complete agreement between the relative seriousness of these types of crimes as rated by the law, the courts, the judges, and the public. The seriousness was also viewed in the same way by different segments of the public, all rank order correlations between sub-groups being higher than 0·95.

What could be the explanation for the sharp contrast between these two studies? Part of the explanation may be found in differences in the choice of method, subjects and cases compared. Most important, perhaps, is the fact that the cases chosen by Makela varied somewhat more as to seriousness than the cases used by Rose and Prell, most of them moreover being related to a common theme, namely drinking. These methodological differences, however, are hardly sufficient to explain all of the contrast. Rather, the different results may be attributed in large measure, to differences between Finland and the United States. While the former is a rather homogeneous society with a high degree of shared values among different segments of the population and little tendency towards change, quite the opposite may be said about the United States. It is a highly heterogeneous society, with a high degree of

111

culture conflict, high mobility and rapid change. Evidence of this was found in the comparison between social groups in the study of Rose and Prell (1955, p. 253f.). The homogeneity of the Finnish society appeared just as clearly in Makela's study from the fact that there were only slight differences between the ratings of the two sexes and almost no differences between different segments of society. The absence of *change* in attitudes (at least at the time of the survey, in 1964) was evident from the fact that the age factor was of no consequence whatsoever for the variables studied (Makela, 1966, p. 42).[8]

A comparison between public opinion about the seriousness of crimes and the seriousness reflected in the Penal Code carried out with a group of students in Stockholm (Linden & Simila, 1969) also showed a high positive correlation (rank order correlation based on minimum penalty compared to rank ordering by students was 0·82).

In conclusion, no clearcut picture emerges concerning the co-variance between law and legal attitudes. Whether they are in agreement or not in a certain society seems to depend upon what society, what time in history, what types of crime we are dealing with, and probably upon several other factors.

The next, and perhaps even more important question we shall have to ask is what is the relationship between legal attitudes and legal behaviour? We have seen that the degree of knowledge about law was not very highly correlated with adherence to law. However, one might expect, as many scholars have, that there is a high correlation between people's acceptance of laws and their legal behaviour. The simplest way of tackling this question is to ask: what are the differences between the legal attitudes of criminals and non-criminals? This question we shall try to answer in the next section.

Attitudes towards law among criminals and non-criminals

Comparative study of the legal and moral attitudes of offenders and non-offenders has attracted many researchers. An important source of inspiration for such studies was one part of the criminological theory of *differential association* (first proposed by Sutherland in 1934). According to this theory, 'a person becomes delinquent because of an excess of definitions favourable to violation of law over definitions unfavourable to violation of law' (Sutherland & Cressey, *Principles of Criminology* 1960, sixth edition, p. 78). If this criterion of criminality were taken literally, it would be easy to construct a questionnaire which could be used to discriminate criminals from non-criminals. This questionnaire should contain equally balanced numbers of positive and negative expressions about law. Whoever subscribed to an excess of negative expression could then be diagnosed as a criminal.

Several authors have indeed taken the theory of differential association rather literally and have used its criterion as a working hypothesis for the construction of questionnaires and research designs along the lines described above. Only one study—in rather special circumstances as we shall see—has in fact obtained distinctly opposing attitudes when comparing criminals and non-criminals. All other comparative studies have shown that the majority of *both criminals and non-criminals* have attitudes that are fairly unfavourable to violation of law. In other words, literally interpreted, this part of the theory of differential association must be rejected. However, many researchers have reformulated the theory, replacing the prediction of an absolute difference with one of a relative difference between criminal and non-criminal attitudes. The criminal is expected to have relatively *more* anti-social and *fewer* pro-social norms than the non-criminals. We shall examine the studies to see to what extent the latter hypothesis has been supported by empirical research.

We shall look first at studies in which comparison has been made between a group of registered offenders (such as juvenile delinquents, or inmates of correctional or reformatory institutions) and a group of 'non-offenders' (in this connection, as a rule, this merely means persons not known to be registered offenders).

Simpson (1934–35) was probably the first one to compare prisoners and non-prisoners. Two hundred inmates in a prison in Illinois and 250 teachers were asked to rate the seriousness of 45 described offences. A comparison showed only slight differences between the two groups. In a study carried out by Christiansen in 1953, comparison was made between the legal knowledge and attitudes of a group of short-term prisoners and a sample of the general population in Copenhagen (Kutchinsky, 1968). Compared to men in the general population, the prisoners were slightly more

113

tolerant towards crime and criminals, but when the prisoners were compared to non-prisoners from the working class only, the differences tended to disappear. Similar results were obtained in a Polish study, comparing legal and moral opinions of prisoners and non-prisoners (Kojder, 1970).

Sechrest (1969) compared the attitudes of prison inmates to the attitudes of the staff and correctional officers in the same prison. The conclusion was that no significant differences between inmates and staff were found as to the ranking of the seriousness of 39 offences. When overall 'scale means' of seriousness were compared, significant differences appeared between the inmate ratings and those of correctional officers and parole agents. The difference between inmates and clinical and administrative staff, however, was slight.

Similar conclusions emerge from a series of studies by Reckless and various co-researchers, comparing attitudes of prisoners and non-prisoners in several countries (Reckless, 1965); Reckless & Ferracuti, 1968; Mylonas & Reckless, 1968; Toro-Calder, Cedeno & Reckless, 1968). Although, in some cases, indices based on selected items could be constructed and could indicate statistically significant differences between prisoners and various general population groups, the conclusion can hardly be avoided that the degree of resemblance rather than of difference was remarkable (see the review of these studies in Kutchinsky, 1972a).

Several studies have been concerned especially with differences between delinquent and non-delinquent boys—the former sometimes being in institutions, sometimes merely 'registered' delinquents. Such studies were carried out in a number of different ways by Durea (1933), Bishop (1940), Chapman (1957), Ball (1957–58), Bjorkenhed (1959), Morris (1965), Shoham & Shaskolsky (1969), and Waldo & Hall (1970). In six of these studies no differences or only slight differences in legal attitudes were found between delinquents and non-delinquents. Only two studies, Bjorkenhed (1959) and Ball (1957–58) yielded results with highly significant differences. It would seem reasonable to take a closer look at these two studies, which seem to form exceptions to a general 'rule'.

Bjorkenhed (1959) compared 300 young delinquent boys with 200 young non-delinquents with regard to general attitudes towards crime. The differences in attitudes found were statistically significant and quite considerable. However, the comparison between the social and educational background of these two groups revealed very
114

significant differences too. No less than 29% of the delinquents had attended schools for backward children, while none of the non-delinquents had been to such schools; only 4% of the delinquent boys were going to high school as against 50% of the non-delinquents; and 42% of the delinquents came from broken homes as against only 10% of the non-delinquents. One cannot ignore the likelihood that these considerable background differences might have been responsible for the extraordinary difference in attitudes. I would expect that in a comparison restricted to those parts of the non-delinquent group whose social background was somewhat closer to that of the delinquents, the difference would disappear or be reduced to a 'normal' level.

This objection cannot be raised against the study by Ball (1957–58). He compared 108 boys incarcerated in a Southern State Reformatory with a sample of 99 public school boys. The two samples were closely matched for age, and according to the author, 'to a lesser extent for intelligence and social–economic status' (p. 261). Both groups filled in a questionnaire with twelve items all having to do with what the author called 'attitude towards the prevalence of stealing'. The author's conclusion that 'the delinquents hold markedly more positive attitudes towards stealing than any of the other groups' (p. 274) seemed justified by the findings. When the scale was dichotomized into 'positive' and 'negative' parts, 71% of the delinquent boys held 'positive' and 29% 'negative' attitudes towards stealing. Among the non-delinquents there was an opposite tendency: 38% held 'positive' and 62% 'negative' attitudes towards stealing (Ball, 1957–58, p. 266). Apparently this study alone supports the literal interpretation of the theory of differential association.

The explanation for this is perhaps to be found in the way in which 'attitudes towards stealing' were investigated. Contrary to all the other studies mentioned, Ball used a 'masked' questionnaire technique in which the respondents were not asked about their own attitudes but about what they thought other people's attitudes would be. Thus the first question was: 'Do you think many people are honest?' As an answer, the respondents were instructed to check one of the following propositions: 'Almost all of them; most of them; some of them; only a few of them; none of them.' Question two was: 'How many people would steal something if they had a good chance?' Here the answer categories were: 'All

115

of them; most of them; about half of them; none of them.' All the rest of the questions were formulated in the same way as question two, with only a few key words being substituted ('taking things', 'steal money', 'steal from a store', and so on). Proponents of this type of 'masked' questionnaire technique believe that the answers given to such questions are indicative of the person's own opinions. In the present case, however, one may have certain doubts that such a 'projection' is taking place. In order to project one's own attitudes onto other people, some degree of identification with others would seem necessary, and I suspect that the incarcerated delinquent would identify 'many people' not with himself, but with 'those outside'. If this suspicion is correct, the findings by Ball do not contradict those of others, for the simple reason that Ball's study deals with something different.

What does Ball's study deal with? In my opinion, there are two ways in which the findings may be interpreted: One interpretation is that by attributing thievish tendencies to 'other people' the delinquent is simply expressing a rejection of these people—he is 'rejecting the rejectors' as phrased by McCorkle & Corn (1954). This interpretation of the findings clearly agrees with the theory of delinquency proposed by Sykes & Matza (1957). According to this theory, delinquents do not commit offences because they have 'delinquent values'—their beliefs about 'right and wrong' are quite similar to those of the general society. Rather, they will tend to '*drift*' into delinquency (Matza, 1964) because their moral beliefs may be temporarily slackened or 'neutralized'. The 'techniques of neutralization' which are provided by the delinquent subcultures, permit them, so to speak, to steal without considering themselves thieves. Sykes & Matza mention five such techniques of neutralization—the fourth one being precisely the one which appears to be at work in the study by Ball. The delinquent is 'condemning the condemners'—'his condemners, he may claim, are hypocrites, deviants in disguise ... By attacking others, the wrongfulness of his own behaviour is more easily repressed or lost from view' (Sykes & Matza, 1957, p. 468).

Quite a different interpretation of the findings by Ball has been suggested by Nettler (1961). Taking the questions in the questionnaire and the answers by the delinquents and non-delinquents at their face value, he suggested that the delinquents were simply expressing a high degree of realism when they answered
116

questions like 'Do you think many people have taken things at some time?' In opposition to the non-delinquents, most of the delinquents gave the answers 'About half', 'Most', or 'All'. Research on self-reported crime has amply proved that the delinquents in Ball's study were right, while the non-delinquents were wrong.

It should be added that there need not be any disagreement between the two interpretations of this finding: neutralization techniques do not necessarily have to be invented out of thin air. On the contrary, the more the 'neutralizing issue' is supported by fact, the more effective it may be expected to be.

Finally, in this context mention should be made of studies in which heterogeneous populations of 'non-criminals' have completed questionnaires, thus permitting internal comparisons between legal attitudes and self-reported delinquency or criminality. One such study by Hindelang (1970) was directly designed to test the 'delinquency and drift' theory of Matza (1964). Sixty-nine juveniles were asked to report on their involvement in 26 delinquent activities. They were also asked to evaluate each activity along an approval–disapproval continuum. For 13 of the 15 delinquent activities that could be analysed, those engaging in the act were significantly more approving of the act than those not engaging in it. The author concluded that the findings did not support Matza's theory which suggests that delinquents and non-delinquents share similar moral prohibitions. It seems to me however that this interpretation of the findings can be disputed. According to the neutralization theory, one would expect persons who had committed a certain act to look more leniently upon it than persons who had not. This would especially be the case with acts that had not been detected, since in such cases, rationalization would still be effective. The break-down, upon detection, of rationalizations supporting criminal activity is a well-known feature (cf. Cressey, 1953, pp. 121ff.).

Clark & Wenninger (1964) gathered data among 1154 public school students in four different communities. They concluded that 'data of several varieties support the hypothesis that involvement in illegal behaviour is associated in some fashion with a negative attitude toward the legal institutions' (p. 188). The relation between legal attitudes and extent of admitted illegal behaviour was expressed in correlation coefficients (Pearsonian r) ranging from

117

0·21 among urban lower class youth to 0·27 in a rural farm district and an industrial city. Although statistically significant, correlations of this size must be considered very modest.

Syren & Tham (1968) compared attitudes towards crime with the amount of self-admitted crime among 478 school children in Sweden. Only a slight positive correlation was found between these two variables. An analysis of variance including a variable called 'relationship to parents' showed, however, that the relationship between 'attitudes towards crime' and 'delinquency' might be explained by this underlying factor. The authors concluded: 'The analysis of the results seems to show that attitudes are without any interest in the study of the causes of delinquency' (Syren & Tham, 1968, p. 53).[9]

Waldo & Hall (1970) offered a rather similar conclusion on the basis of data from 627 7th-grade boys in nine junior high schools. Teachers or school principals classified the respondents into non-delinquent groups and groups of delinquents or juveniles with a high delinquency potential. The authors concluded that the data offered tentative support for the hypothesis that there was a certain relationship between attitudes towards the criminal justice system and delinquency. 'However, the relationship is not very strong and would not explain very much of the variation in the dependent variables' (p. 298).

The empirical evidence presented in this section leads to the conclusion that, generally speaking, criminals and non-criminals, delinquents and non-delinquets, persons who have committed crimes and persons who have not, share more or less the same legal attitudes, as expressed in questionnaire studies. Contrary to expectations criminals apparently do not have criminal attitudes—they are, at best, slightly more tolerant towards crimes than non-criminals.

I would like to mention three different ways of interpreting this finding. The first one is in line with the objections that can be raised against attitude surveys in general, and especially when applied to groups of criminals. There is something paradoxical in an attempt to demonstrate some persons' 'fundamentally anti-social norms' by asking them to give *honest* replies to a questionnaire about these norms. In other words, the apparent similarity between the attitudes of 'lawful citizens' and 'criminals' may be a product of the simple fact that the criminals give dishonest replies,

118

that they pretend to be more lawful than they actually are. They may do so deliberately or more unconsciously for several reasons: because they are 'habitual liars', because they want to impress the interviewer, because they are submissive to the expectations of the interviewer, or because they suspect that the promises of anonymity are fake and that honest answers might harm their possibilities for parole, or might lead to arrest. Another possibility is that, broadly speaking, criminals share such legal attitudes with the general population, but that in both cases it is a matter of very *superficial* veneer—a set of conventional opinions which everybody can make a show of. You cannot tell the criminals from the non-criminals by such superficial expressions of attitudes just as you cannot tell the difference between a criminal and a non-criminal from his appearance.

Upon closer inspection, however, these attempts to explain away the results of the comparisons between criminals and non-criminals, as well as the very hypotheses of some of the studies, appear to be based on a rather dubious assumption. It is considered a truism that it is possible to distinguish qualitatively between criminals and non-criminals. In principle, the difference is supposed to be there, just as self-evidently as for instance the difference between men and women—finding the *criteria* for the distinction merely being a technical challenge.

However, a decade of heavy research on self-declared crime has shown that with regard to legal behaviour, there is, at best, only a quantitative difference between so-called criminals and non-criminals. Such research raises a third possibility: that it would be reasonable to expect what we have in fact found, namely that there is only a small quantitative difference between the legal attitudes of so-called criminals and non-criminals. Indeed, common sense would seem to lead to the same conclusion. Assuming that there *is* a direct relationship between legal behaviour and legal attitudes, the expectation would be that 'persistent criminal attitudes' would be correlated with 'persistent criminal behaviour'. However, scarcely anyone believes that a person convicted of having committed a few criminal acts (or admitting in a questionnaire to the commission of such acts) should be consistently criminal in his behaviour. A criminal, of course, does not violate *all* legal regulations *all* the time, rather he is a quite ordinary 'lawful citizen' most of the time. For that reason also, there is not the slightest grounds

119

for expecting that 'criminals' should not have 'quite ordinary lawful opinions'.

This does not mean that I would deny the existence of persons who are rather persistently 'anti-social' in their behaviour as well as their attitudes. Such persons, however, remain the exception. Moreover, they may be found both among groups who are registered and groups who are not registered as criminals. These persons form one end of a *continuum* which at the other extreme has the similarly rare group of persons who are consistently conformist in both behaviour and attitudes. The vast majority of citizens, including the majority of those in correctional institutions, are in between, both with regard to attitudes and behaviour. In other words, with regard to general attitudes towards crime among offenders and non-offenders we have found what we might well have expected: a picture dominated by the lack of differences.

We may then proceed to look at such differences as there were. First of all, we found an overall tendency among criminals, or persons who had committed criminal offences, to be slightly more tolerant towards crime and criminals, to believe somewhat more often that punishments are too severe, that the police and courts do not treat all citizens alike, that criminality is more widespread than most people think, and so on. In many cases, it would seem that these opinions about punishments, legal institutions and other people are rather realistic: they may be a result of the direct experience of these groups. Undoubtedly, one may find very similar opinions among many criminologists.

That these opinions are somewhat more realistic and less naive than those of 'ordinary citizens' does not mean that they may not be interpreted in some sense as being more 'favourable towards the violation of laws'. It is just possible that a slightly less naive view of the realities of social control (e.g. that a person who commits a crime does not automatically become a 'criminal', that crime *does* very often pay, or that equality does not always prevail in the justice system) may be *one* of the factors facilitating the use of illegal behaviour in a situation of choice. However, whether such opinions about crimes and criminal justice are labelled as *criminal*, *tolerant*, or *realistic*, the studies reviewed in this section have clearly demonstrated that having such attitudes is neither a necessary nor a sufficient condition for committing crimes, or becoming a convict.

120

The relevance of sex, age, education, and some other 'social' factors

As we have seen, the fact that a person may be classified, in one way or another, as 'a criminal' is of little consequence, generally speaking, for his legal attitudes. Yet we know that people do have very different attitudes. What factors are responsible for these differences? What *are* the determinants of legal attitudes? In this and in the following two sections, these questions will be pursued.

When Segerstedt, Karlsson, & Rundbland (1949) made their pioneer study on 'the general sense of justice', they defined their aim in the following way: '(1) to measure the attitudes forming the general sense of justice, and (2) to trace the attitudes back to special social groups' (p. 325). 'Social group' was defined as 'people behaving in a uniform way because of common codes' (p. 325). In order to trace these groups Segerstedt used traditional sociological criteria, such as sex, age, social status, urbanization, marital status, religious affiliation, etc. He knew very well that categories obtained through these criteria were not themselves identical with the social groups looked for. It was expected, however, that they would serve as 'divining-rods', indicating directions for further research into the sources of the various social norms.

Several later students have pursued the same aim as Segerstedt. It is impossible to go into much detail as regards the data obtained. In what follows therefore there is some concentration on the three traditionally most important areas (sex, age, and level of education), and only brief mention of some others. The review of these factors will by necessity contain many generalizations and little documentation. But generalizations are derived from the findings of several studies on KOL,[10] and whenever a statement is undocumented and unqualified, it means that the conclusion was supported by several studies and contradicted by none.

The sex factor. Most studies in which men and women have been questioned show some differences in attitudes between the two sexes (one exception was the study of Mathieson (1965)). However, conspicuously few of the differences found in *some* studies remain unopposed by findings in other studies. And even in those studies where differences are found, these tend to disappear in some categories, when crossed with other variables such as level of

121

education. Before mentioning the differences that have been fairly well substantiated and remained fairly unquestioned, one very clear and modifying tendency should be noted: Whatever differences are found between men and women, these *differences tend to disappear with younger age groups, with increasing urbanization, with increasing social and educational level, and in newer studies.*

The most solid difference found in KOL studies was that women tend to have less *knowledge* about law and similar subjects than men. This tendency was even found on the higher educational level. As to *attitudes*, the general tendency is towards a considerable similarity between men's and women's opinions about the seriousness of crimes. Differences only appear when we probe further. Thus a tendency found in several studies was that when dealing with the topic on a highly *abstract* level such as expressing opinion about the severity of punishments in general, women tended to be more severe or intolerant than men, while on a *concrete* level (e.g. when meting out punishment for a concrete crime) women would tend to be more lenient than men. Related to this finding was a slight tendency towards women having not only somewhat more conformist, and morally disapproving attitudes (which would be dominant on the abstract level) but also more emotional, and more socially and personally minded attitudes (which would tend to dominate when a particular offender and his fate came into the picture).

Several studies showed a slight tendency for men to consider crimes of property more seriously than women did. Differences between the attitudes of men and women were also found in relation to moral offences, specially sex crimes. These differences, however, depended strongly upon the ages of the respondents *and* upon the dates of the studies. Women in earlier studies, and older women in newer studies tended to be more severe than men with regard to these types of offences. Among young persons, however, and especially in newer studies, there was a tendency in the *opposite* direction.

Kaupen *et al.* (1971) divided the female respondents into two categories: housewives and women who worked outside the home ('working women'). The findings were that wherever there were differences between men and women (in most cases there were no differences) the attitudes of the 'working women' were sometimes similar to those of the men and sometimes similar to those

122

of the housewives. The *types* of questions in which the 'working women' sometimes followed the men and sometimes the housewives were rather suggestive. They tentatively indicate, together with some other studies, that the differences generally found between the sexes may be related to two rather independent underlying factors:

(1) *The specific gender role patterns* which are imposed through upbringing and education from a very tender age, will tend to cause certain deep-rooted differences between boys and girls, and between men and women. These patterns may be slowly changing through the generations, but will remain more or less unchanged throughout the life of the individual.

(2) *The degree of social participation* starts being different for boys and girls usually from the end of their compulsory school education. From then on, men tend to become increasingly more engaged in public affairs, as well as in social life in general than women. This fact may be expected to have certain direct influences on attitudes and behaviour. To the degree that women do participate socially on the same level as men, such attitudinal differences will disappear rather quickly. There are certain indications that, perhaps as part of this social participation, women on the highest levels of education will tend to overcompensate for the attitude differences inherent in the sexual patterns, with the result that they adopt attitudes that are 'more male' than the men's (see Kutchinsky, 1968, p. 138ff.).

Age. This has appeared to be of relevance in all studies having data about this factor, except that of Makela. The *general* trends can be summarized as follows: Young persons tend to be more lenient, tolerant, reform-minded and liberal towards crime and criminals, while older people tend to be more severe, intolerant, oppressive and conservative with regard to legal reforms. Young persons also tend to express less respect for the law than older persons. One study (Versele, 1971) showed that young people generally had more knowledge about law than older people. Two important points should be added to this general conclusion. Firstly, in early studies (mainly before 1965) the age differences were less prominent than in the more recent studies. Secondly, the differences between older and younger *women* seem to be much more prominent than the differences between older and younger

123

men. In other words, the findings suggest that the differences between young and old people are becoming more distinct, and this tendency towards polarization is more marked among women than among men.

That older persons tend to be more conservative and strict while younger ones often have more liberal and reformist attitudes is a well known phenomenon, which is traditionally explained as being essentially a matter of age: people tend to lose the 'revolutionary' attitudes of youth and become more 'conservative and responsible' as they grow older. This explanation, however, does not square very well with the apparently *widening* generation gap, since the implication would be that the process of 'growing old' should cause *greater* attitude changes today than some years ago. Similarly, one would also have to explain why 'growing old' should have a stronger influence on women's attitudes than on men's. Although one could perhaps find ways of explaining such time changes and sex differences in the light of a theory of 'growing conservative with age', I believe that the following explanation of age differences is more consistent with the findings.

This explanation starts from the assumption that in many contemporary societies, certain changes of values are taking place which tend to influence almost everybody. The change may be regarded as a movement in a certain direction and with a certain general speed. The direction is more or less the same for everybody, but the speed differs considerably in different sections of the population. While younger persons will adapt to the changing values more easily (some of them may even be taking the lead) older persons will tend to move less rapidly (some of them may even tend to try jamming on the brakes). According to this assumption, the process of growing old does not directly influence people's *attitudes* in any way. What 'growing old' means in this connection is 'becoming increasingly less susceptible to influences'. People do not grow more conservative or intolerant—it is society which is moving away from their viewpoints. In agreement with this, the explanation for the increasing polarization between old and young persons is that society as a whole is changing more rapidly today than it did earlier. Similarly, the reason for the greater difference in attitudes between younger and older women than between younger and older men is that the views of women are changing more rapidly than those of men. (See also Kutchinsky, 1972.)

124

Education. This appears to be an important discriminating factor in all studies where such data is available. Indeed several studies indicate that in certain respects, level of education is more important in determining attitudes than socio-economic factors (Kutchinsky, 1966; Blom, 1968). However, the findings about the impact of the education factor are still somewhat contradictory. While Mathiesen (1965) and Kutchinsky (1966) found an increasing intolerance towards crimes—in the form of increasing punitive demands—with rising educational level in two *Norwegian* studies (carried out in 1961 and 1962), Podgorecki (1966a, 1970) found the opposite tendency in a *Polish* study. In both the Norwegian and the Polish studies there were some modifications to this general tendency which might explain, in part, the apparent contradictory. In the Norwegian study, along with increasing punitiveness, there was an increasing demand for psychiatric *treatment* of offenders. In the Polish study, persons with a higher education would tend to be more severe than persons of lower education with regard to 'infringements of the norms of order, use of property, or of elementary norms of social co-existence' (Podgorecki, 1970, p. 12 and the preceding paper. Similarly, Versele (1971) found that higher educational level led to an increase in the opinion that it is a duty of the courts both to protect society and to help the offender. Since both Versele (1971) and Blom (1968) found level of education positively correlated with *confidence* in the legal system, a reasonable conclusion would seem to be that education influences people towards greater identification with the legal authorities and towards advocating various 'rational' measures for the maintenance of social order.

This conclusion has been supported by a comparison between the above-mentioned Norwegian study (in 1961) and a similar Danish one, data from which only recently became available.[11] Although both of these studies were actually concerned with self-declared criminality, they both had one question asking the respondents (in both studies male conscripts) what in general they thought about the severity of punishments in their country. The results showed that 67% of the Norwegian conscripts as against 43% of the Danish conscripts thought that punishments were too lenient (only 3% and 5%, respectively, found punishments too severe, while the remainder would either consider punishments adequate, or would refuse to answer the question). When these results were related to the respondents' level of education, a striking difference appeared. While the Norwegian study showed that with increasing level of education there was a steadily increasing percentage who considered punishments too lenient, the opposite tendency was present in the Danish study. Among the conscripts at the lowest level of education (primary school only) 51% in Norway and 45% in Denmark found punishment too lenient. Among conscripts at the highest level of education ('studentereksamen') 72% in Norway as against only 29% in Denmark considered punishments too lenient. This finding agrees with another comparison between these two studies which showed that the relation between attitudes and the degree of *urbanization* was also opposite in Norway and Denmark. In Denmark the city population had less severe attitudes than the rural population; in Norway it was vice versa.

It seems reasonable to interpret both of these findings in accordance with the 'theory of imitation', originated by Tarde (1890). According to Tarde, influences concerning behaviour and ideologies tend to move 'downward' from the higher to the lower social strata, and from urban to rural districts. In the light of this theory discrepancies in legal attitudes related to education as well as to area of residence may be taken as an indication that changes are taking place or will take place in the near future in the legal system. The direction of the change will be indicated by the trend which appears when going from the lower educational level to the higher ones and from rural to urban districts. In accordance with this, one would predict, on the basis of the two studies mentioned, that the sanctioning system in Norway should be moving in the direction of more severe punishments while the opposite trend should be expected in Denmark. Indeed recent developments in the two countries over the past years have confirmed both of these 'predictions'.

Other social variables. Let me just touch briefly upon some of the other more or less traditional 'sociological variables'. The degree of *urbanization* was already mentioned in one connection. The general tendency in most studies is that people in rural districts are more intolerant towards crimes than people in urban districts. In Poland there was no difference, and in Norway, as we have seen, the tendency was in the opposite direction. *Religious* as
126

well as *political* affiliation tend to show little differentiation, except in the case of people belonging to extreme wings. The *socio-economic* variables are difficult to deal with (see Kutchinsky, 1972). A general tendency found in most studies was that persons from higher social strata were generally more repressive and intolerant towards crimes than persons from lower social strata. Higher social levels were especially intolerant towards crimes of property and violence, and towards very serious offences. On the other hand, Segerstedt *et al.* (1949) found higher social groups more tolerant towards homosexuality. In most studies there was also a clear tendency that persons from higher social levels have more *confidence* in the judicial authorities.

One of the problems of using the traditional sociological variables as 'divining rods' when trying to trace the origins of legal attitudes is that they are quite often too coarse. When dividing people according to such criteria, one often happens to lump together persons who have, in fact, very little in common. It is not very likely, for instance, that a landowner and a stableman share the same attitudes, although both belong to the rural population. Similarly, a skilled factory worker and a small freeholder may have the same income, but still have quite opposite views on many questions.

In an attempt to avoid this problem, several KOL studies have departed from the usual demand for a representative quota sample of the 'general population'. Instead (or sometimes in addition) they have used purposive samples of members of *specific groups* such as policemen, blue-collar workers, farmers, doctors, etc. For example using such a sampling technique Van Houtte (1970) was able to show that a person's attitude towards tax evasion would depend very much on his own opportunity to avoid reporting income to the tax authorities. Liberal professions and doctors were much more permissive with regard to tax evasion than wage earners, regardless of income level. The general tendency was that the greater the opportunity of having 'hidden income', the less the disapproval of tax evasion.

Two persons belonging to the same nationality, sex, age, level of education, etc., or belonging to the same sub-cultural environment, may nevertheless have entirely different attitudes. This common sense fact sometimes surprises social scientists who are accustomed to considering groups as units. The *individual* differences are therefore often treated as chance factors—this is what sociologists usually do with factors which, for some reason or other, they cannot adequately control or obtain information about. One may, however, in different ways try to find the 'sources', or at least some common denominators among these variables in the *psychological* background or the *personality* of the subjects. There are many different ways of obtaining such information ranging from adding one or a few psychological questions to the questionnaire, or using special 'personality inventories', to intensive 'depth interviews'.

Using questions from a personality inventory, Podgorecki (1966a, 1970) found that personality factors were very important in determining legal attitudes. Thus, the following psychological factors would 'lead to greater rigorism: ... feelings of insecurity, social adjustment, feelings of frustration' (Podgorecki, 1966a, p. 90). Conversely, factors leading to greater tolerance were: 'Absence of a feeling of insecurity, wider social contacts, mild upbringing' etc. (p. 90). These psychological factors were not only independent of the sociological background factors (education, occupation, etc.), they were also usually more important than these in determining attitudes.

Kutchinsky (1970b) used a variety of *non-statistical* methods (including intensive, non-structured interviews and the so-called 'projective techniques'). The purpose of these studies was not primarily to find personality variables which might be determinants of legal attitudes, but rather to analyse the position and formation of these attitudes within the frame work of the personality set-up. The main conclusions could be summarized as follows: '... most people do not have one solid and consistent set of attitudes, rather within the same individual there exists several different layers of attitudes. Furthermore, there may very well be a contradiction between the attitudes in one layer and apparently similar attitudes in another layer ... One person may be speaking in a very tolerant way, expressing very liberal attitudes towards many things,
128

when suddenly some extremely intolerant and repressive traits appear. It is interesting to observe that most subjects are not at all bothered by these inconsistencies in their utterances. If someone happens to feel uncomfortable about it he or she will usually come up with a number of rationalizations so that an apparent harmony is secured, (Kutchinsky, 1970b, p. 10f.). There is hardly any doubt that the attitudes expressed in a survey belong to the 'surface layer' of personality. This does not mean, however, that such attitudes are not important parts of the personality (just as the skin is an important part of the body). Moreover, surface opinions may derive their content and direction from the deepest motivational layers in personality, although very often in a most complicated way.

Studies of attitude change

In the foregoing sections I have suggested that differences between some categories of respondents in respect to certain attitudes may be interpreted as reflections of recent attitude changes in society as a whole (and to some extent even future changes in the legal system). In the present section, I shall deal with studies directly concerned with observing changes in legal attitudes. Such studies may be divided into two rather different types: studies of *short-term changes* and studies of *long-term changes*. While only the latter may yield information about real changes that have taken place in the legal culture, the former type of investigation may tell us something about the *ways* in which these influencing processes occur.

Short-term changes of attitudes are usually studied in experimental settings. The usual procedure is for attitudes to be measured twice, with an interval lasting from a few minutes to a few weeks, with some kind of stimulation hypothesized to affect the attitudes being applied during the intervening period. One of the earliest studies on attitudes towards crimes was an experiment of this type. In 1931 Thurstone used the method of paired comparisons in a before and after experiment designed to assess the influence of a motion picture about 'gambling' on children's assessment of the word 'gambler'. A questionnaire in which 13 types of offences

129

(including gambling) were presented in pairs was completed by 240 school children before and after a motion picture which had featured a gambler as the main character. It appeared that the motion picture resulted in a very strong displacement of the word 'gambler' on the scale in a more serious direction. Thurstone interpreted this as a result of a cognitive change, i.e. the children's conception of what 'gambling' meant had changed rather than their attitude towards the particular person. (Similar experiments on attitude changes by Walker & Argyle (1964) and Berkowitz & Walker (1967) on the effects of 'awareness of law' on moral judgements have already been referred to (p. 106).

Kutchinsky (1972b) studied the effect of pornography on attitudes towards sex crimes. Seventy subjects divided into three groups were pretested with a questionnaire called SIKOL[12] which was then followed by a one-hour stimulation with pornographic literature, magazines and films. One group was retested immediately after the stimulation, a second group was retested after four days and a third group after two weeks. The author concluded that while there might have been an effect in individual cases, the pornography, generally speaking, did not have any influence on the subjects' attitudes towards sex crimes.

The second type of study on changes of attitudes are the studies of *long-term changes*. It would seem that an excellent opportunity for conducting such studies would be to utilize the 'natural experimental conditions' created by amendments to laws or the introduction of new laws. So far, however, this type of study has only been carried out a few times. The follow-up study on the effects of the Norwegian Housemaid Law described by Aubert (1966) is probably the best known among these (see the more detailed discussion above on p. 104). This study was not a real 'before and after study', since the first part was carried out shortly *after* the introduction of the new law, while the follow-up took place six years later. In this case, however, such a procedure was justified since the conditions, which the new law was intended to control, had not by any means been affected by the law when the first investigation took place. The conclusion of the follow-up study was that the major source of influence on knowledge and attitudes with regard to the housemaid law was the influence of friends and relatives. This influence appeared to be much stronger than that of the mass media. Attention should however be drawn to the fact that at

130

the time of the Norwegian study *television* had not yet been introduced. Another reason for the relative lack of influence of the mass media may be the fact that, although the Housemaid Law was occasionally mentioned in the press and on the radio, it was hardly a big issue. One might expect that attitude changes in relation to laws which have been widely publicized in the press are more likely to be influenced by the mass media. In such cases the influence of the mass media, especially the television, is inseparable from the peer influence. The media usually inspire and inform discussions among peers, thus being indirectly a source of influence.

Two findings reported by Kutchinsky (1973) point towards the correctness of this assumption. A comparison between Gallup survey data before and after the repeal of the ban on pornographic literature and pictures in Denmark in 1967 and 1969, respectively, showed that a considerable change in public opinion had taken place in the course of the period around the repeal. In 1965, 46% of the total population were in favour of repeal of the ban on pornographic *writings*. One year after the repeal, in 1968, the percentage in favour of the repeal had increased to 61%. Similarly, in 1968, 49% were in favour of a repeal of the ban on pornographic *pictures*. In 1970, i.e. one year after the repeal, 57% declared that they were in favour of this decision. A rapid change in public opinion as indicated here could hardly have taken place without the influence of the mass media, which, with few exceptions, publicized the parliamentary decision as well as the effect of the repeal very favourably.

Similar results were found in an 'after-only' survey on attitudes towards sex crimes. Kutchinsky (1973) tried to assess the degree of possible changes in attitudes of the adult Copenhagen population concerning different types of sex crimes, and sex crimes in general. Using various techniques of questioning and data processing, he arrived at the conclusion that a considerable change in attitudes had indeed taken place with regard to certain types of minor sex crimes (see above p. 108). When asked about the sources of the change, the mass media were mentioned by 29% of those who had changed, while 'associates' were only mentioned by 10%. As far as we can trust people's own opinion about what influences them, in this case the change was more often due to mass media than to the influence of peers. This accords very well with the fact that a sex crime receives rather more attention in the mass media

131

than, for instance, a violation of the Housemaid Law.

The finding of a considerable change in attitudes towards sex crimes, especially among women, was also a main feature of the only study available, in which a survey has been meticulously replicated after several years. What was probably the first study on legal attitudes, by Thurstone (1927), was repeated 40 years later by Coombs (1967). In both cases, the subjects were college students from Chicago (which, of course, means that they were not representative of public opinion in general), and in both cases the same stimulus material (19 different crimes) and the same method ('paired comparison') was utilized. The results included some very interesting findings. Thurstone (1927) had already shown that three categories of offences formed separate 'clusters' on the scale: injury to the person, sex offences and property offences. The study 40 years later showed that sex crimes had come to be looked upon much less seriously, while crimes of violence against the person had changed in a much more serious direction. The latter finding agrees with the assumptions of McClintock (1963, p. 69) and Christie (1971). Concerning property offences the attitudes had changed in some cases while they had remained unchanged in others. It was especially notable while attitudes towards burglary and larceny had remained unchanged, students had come to look much more leniently upon 'receiving stolen goods'. That this offence is, in fact, considered by modern college students of both sexes (in the United States) to be a rather innocent act may explain the apparent ease with which an increasing number of thieves get rid of 'the goods'.

Conclusion

In this article I have tried to provide some answers to the question: What is known, at the moment, about the so-called legal consciousness of the common man? The answers are to a large extent based on fairly 'soft' research, very often at early and exploratory stages. Many of the conclusions, therefore, can only be provisional. The study of knowledge and opinion about law, however, is an area of research in rapid progress. In the fairly near future, much more substantial answers will be available—not least through a series of cross-national studies which are now being put

132

into operation. Apart from mentioning some facts about the actual contents of the legal knowledge and opinion in various countries, I have also dealt with some factors determining these conceptions, and with their relationship to legal behaviour. It very soon became clear that 'law' is emphatically not the only factor determining the legal knowledge and attitudes of the public. In fact, under certain conditions (in some countries, and concerning some laws) there is very little agreement between the law and related public opinion. What determines legal attitudes, generally speaking, is a number of cultural, sociological and psychological factors (see 'the three-step hypothesis' of Podgorecki). Among these factors we have seen the importance of national/cultural differences of sex, age, level of education, place of living, and membership of specific interest groups. Finally, we have seen that great importance must be attached to various factors in the psychological background and the personality of the individual. We have also briefly discussed some sources and channels of influence, such as peers and the mass media. Needless to say, the influence of the various factors differ very much from one person to another and from one type of attitude to another. Moreover, it is obvious that only in theory and in statistical analyses can these various determinants be singled out. In the formation of the legal consciousness of the individual they are often inseparately combined and mutually dependent.

More interesting, perhaps, than discussing what factors may be considered determinants (at least in a statistical sense) of legal attitudes is the question: What do legal attitudes themselves determine? Or more broadly formulated: What kinds of useful information can we get through studying legal attitudes? The greatest expectations about the usefulness of KOL research came perhaps from those who thought that these techniques could be used to predict criminal behaviour. These hopes were not fulfilled. As we have seen there is no clearcut relationship between knowledge and attitudes regarding law and adherence to laws. Undoubtedly, research in this area will go on—some scholars are still optimistic about the prospects of being able to predict future criminality by means of more sophisticated attitude questionnaires. Personally, I have doubts about these prospects.

The lack of correlation between criminal attitudes and criminal behaviour does not mean, however, that KOL studies cannot be

133

used in criminological research, i.e. research on the causes and the prevention of crime. On the contrary, I believe that it can become a very successful tool in this area of research. First of all, KOL surveys can very easily be combined with surveys on *victimization* and on *self-reported crime* through which rather direct information on criminality may be obtained. In fact, there is no reason to keep these three closely related areas of research separated.[13] Secondly, there are types of legal behaviour which are much more closely related to legal knowledge and attitudes than the act of committing or abstaining from committing crimes. I am thinking of the various types of *reactions to criminality*, as well as to legislation, law enforcement, and legal authorities. As an example, studies on victims' or potential victims' attitudes towards crimes, towards the offenders, and towards reporting to the police have supplied important information for the interpretation of crime statistics, and studies of attitudes towards criminals have yielded information which may lead to progress in rehabilitation of earlier offenders.

Above all, however, KOL research is a vital part of the sociology of law. The functioning of law in society cannot be properly studied without continuing research into the public image of law, the legal conceptions, the knowledge and opinion of those who are not only being controlled by the law, but who should also be the controllers of law. These are the directions in which modern KOL research is moving.

NOTES

1. The word KOL (*Knowledge* and *Opinion* about *Law*) was coined in conjunction with the establishment of an International research group with the purpose of promoting cross-national research in this area.
2. This article is partly based on the author's more extensive report to the Ninth Conference of Directors of Criminological Research Institutes sponsored by the Council of Europe in December, 1971 (Kutchinsky, 1972).
3. It is necessary to distinguish between two rather different concepts, both of which are usually referred to as 'knowledge about law'. '*Law awareness*' refers to awareness of the very fact that a certain type of behaviour is regulated by law. '*Law acquaintance*' or '*norm acquaintance*' refers to the amount of information a person has about the content matter of a certain normative regulation. These two types of 'legal knowledge' are theoretically independent of each other. For instance, a person may have very specific ideas about how to behave in a certain situation without

134

being aware that this behaviour agrees, or disagrees, with a certain law. On the other hand, a person may be well aware that there is a law regulating a certain type of behaviour but he may have a poor or even false knowledge about the contents of the law.

4. This finding is in striking contrast to an assumption made by Olivecrona (1940), the legal philosopher, as part of an argument concerning the effectiveness of law: 'It is a rather natural element in the fund of knowledge possessed by every adult normal person ... that the law is established by the King and Parliament in certain definite forms' (p. 64).

5. This argument, among others, was used by opponents to the Wolfenden Committee's (1957) recommendation that homosexual behaviour between consenting adults should no longer be a criminal offence in Britain.

6. As might be expected, however, there was a considerable difference in the *variance* of the punitive demands of the judges and the public. The variances (s^2) of the public were generally five to ten times as large as those of the judges. This fact, according to Makela (1966), gives some idea of the gain of uniformity of judicial practice obtained by having professionally trained judges instead of lay judges selected by lot from the whole population.

7. The following correlations coefficients (Rho) were not computed by Makela (who used his findings for another purpose), but by the present author on the basis of Makela's data.

8. The relationship between age differences and attitude change is discussed later (p. 123).

9. The study by Syren & Tham, 1968 (published only in the Swedish language) has been reviewed more thoroughly in Kutchinsky (1970a, pp. 75–77).

10. The conclusions are mainly based on the general studies on KOL reported by Blom (1968), Kaupen, Volks, & Werle (1971), Mathiesen (1965), Makela (1966), Prodgorecki (1966a), Segerstedt et al. (1949), and Kutchinsky (1968, 1970b, 1970c).

11. In both studies large nation-wide sample of male conscripts were questioned anonymously by means of questionnaires. The Norwegian study was carried out in 1961 (N=3028), the Danish one in 1964 (N=7203).

12. The letters in SIKOL stand for *S*pecial *I*nstrument for the study of *K*nowledge and *O*pinion about *L*aw (see Kutchinsky, 1973).

13. Recently, an impressive effort to collect all available material in these three areas of research has been made by the Bureau of Social Science Research, Washington D.C. (Biderman, Oldham, Ward & Eby, 1971).

REFERENCES

Aubert, V.: *Priskontrol og rasjonering. En retssosiologisk forstudie.* Oslo, 1950. (Stencil).
Aubert, V.: *Om straffens sosiale funksjon.* Oslo: Akademisk Forlag, 1954.
Aubert, V.: Some social functions of legislation. *Acta Sociologica,* 1966, *10,* 98–120.
Aubert, V., Eckhoff, T., & Sveri, K.: *En lov i søkelyset. Socialpsykologisk undersøkelse av den norske hushjelplov.* Oslo: Akademisk Forlag, 1952.

Ball, John C.: Delinquent and non-deliquent attitudes toward the prevalence of stealing. *Journal of Criminal Law, Criminology and Police Science*, 1957–58, *48*, 259–274.

Berkowitz, L., & Walker N.: Laws and moral judgements. *Sociometry*, 1967, *30*, 410–422.

Biderman, Albert D., Oldham, Susan S., Ward, Sally K., & Eby, Maureen A.: Interim report on an inventory of surveys of the public on crime, justice and related topics. Bureau of Social Science Research, Inc. 1200 Seventeenth Street, N.W. Washington, D.C. 20036. 1971 (Mimeo.).

Bishop, Ruth: Points of neutrality in social attitudes of delinquents and non-delinquents. *Psychometrica*, 1940, *5*, 35–45.

Björkenhed, Sten: *Ungdom och brott—en attitydundersøkning.* Lund, 1959.

Blom, R.: Contentual differentiation of penalty demands and expectations with regard to justice. University of Tampere, Institute of Sociology, 1968. (Mimeographed).

Christie, Nils: Vold og samfunnsstruktur. I: *Festskrift til Stephan Hurwitz.* København: Juristforbundets Forlag, 1971, pp. 155–177.

Clark, J. P., Wenninger, E. P.: The attitude of juveniles towards the legal institution. *Journal of Criminal Law, Criminology and Police Science*, 1964, *55*, 482–489.

Cressey, Donald R.: *Other people's money.* Glencoe, Illinois: The Free Press, 1953.

Durea, M. A.: An experimental study of attitudes towards juvenile delinquency. *Journal of Applied Psychology*, 1933, *17*, 522–534.

Ehrlich, Eugen: *Grundlegung der Soziologie des Rechts.* München & Leipzig, 1913.

Hindelang, Michael J.: The commitment of delinquents to their misdeeds: Do delinquents drift? *Social Problems*, 1970, *17*, 502–509.

Innstilling til lov om arbeidsvilkår for hushjelp m. fl. fra Hushjelpkomiteen oppnevnt ved. kgl. res. av. 8 oktober 1954. Oslo: Kommunal- og arbeidsdepartementet, 1960.

Kaupen, Wolfgang, Volks, Holger & Werle, Raymund: Compendium of results of a representative survey among the German population on knowledge and opinion of law and legal institutions (KOL). Arbeitskreis für Rechtssoziologie an der Universität zu Köln, 1971.

Kojder, A.: Poglady Prawne i Moralne Recydywistow (Legal and moral opinion of recidivists). In: A Podgorecki, J. Kurozewski, J. Kwasniewski, & M. Łos: *Prawne i Moralne Poglady Spoteczenziwa Polskiego* (Legal and moral opinions of the Polish population). Warszawa 1970.

Kulcsár, K.: The law and the public in Hungary, *Acta Juridica Academiae Scientiarum Hungaricae*, 1968, *10*, 37–62.

Kutchinsky, Berl: Law and education: Some aspects of Scandinavian studies on 'the general sense of justice'. *Acta Sociologica*, 1966, *10*, 21–41.

Kutchinsky, Berl: Knowledge and attitudes regarding legal phenomena in Denmark. In: N. Christie (Ed.): *Scandinavian Studies in Criminology*, *Vol. 2.* Oslo: Universitetsforlaget, 1968. pp. 125–159.

Kutchinsky, Berl: Advances in Scandinavian studies on knowledge and opinion about law. In: *Rechtssociologie en Jurimetri.* Deventer, Holland: Kluwer, 1970. pp. 71–82. (a).

Kutchinsky, Berl: Dan–68. A new series of Danish investigations on Knowledge and Opinion about Law (KOL). A situational report. Paper

136

presented at *the 7th World Congress of Sociology*, Varna 1970. (b).

Kutchinsky, Berl: *Den almindelige retszevidsthed. To danske undersøgelser vedrørende kendskab og holdninger til kriminalitet og retsudøvelse.* Stockholm: Almqvist & Wiksell, 1970. (c).

Kutchinsky, Berl: The perception of deviance: A survey of empirical research. In Report of the Ninth Conference of Directors of Criminological Institutes: Perception of Deviance and Criminality. Strasbourg: Council of Europe, 1972, pp. 10–80, 186–203. (Mimeo).

Kutchinsky, Berl: *Pornography and sex crimes in Denmark. Early research findings.* London: Martin Robertson, 1973. (In press).

Lindén, Per-Anders & Similä, Matti: 'Det almänna rättsmädvetandet' blandt studenter i Stockholm. 3-betygsuppsats i sociologi. Universitetet i Stockholm, 1969. pp. 65 plus appendices. (Stencil).

Mathiesen, T.: *Tiltak mot ungdomskriminalitet. En opinionsundersøkelse.* Oslo: Universitetsforlaget, 1965.

Matza, David: *Delinquency and drift,* New York: John Wiley, 1964.

McClintock, F. H.: *Crimes of violence. Cambridge Studies in Criminology, Vol. 18.* London: Macmillan, 1963.

McCorkle, Lloyd W. & Corn, Richard: Resocialisation within walls. *The Annals of the American Academy of Political and Social Science.* 1954, 293 (May), 88–98.

Morris, Ruth R.: Attitudes towards delinquency by delinquents and their friends. *British Journal of Criminology,* 1965, *5,* 249–265.

Mylonas, Anastassios D. & Reckless, Walter C.: Attitudes toward law enforcement in Greece and the United States. *Journal of Research in Crime and Delinquency,* 1968, *5* (1), 81–88.

Mäkelä, Klaus: Public sense of justice and judicial practice. *Acta Sociologica,* 1966, *10,* 42–67.

Nettler, Gwynn: Good men, bad men, and the perception of reality. *Sociometry,* 1961, *24,* 279–294.

Olivecrona, Karl: *Om lagen och staten.* Lund: Gleerup, 1940.

Podgorecki, A.: The prestige of law. (Preliminary research results). In: Britt-Mari Persson Blegvad (Ed.): *Contributions to the Sociology of Law.* Copenhagen: Munksgaard, 1966. pp. 81–96. (a).

Podgorecki, Adam: The three-step hypothesis on the functioning of the law. Paper presented at the Sixth World Congress of Sociology, Evian, 1966. (Stencil). (b).

Podgorecki, Adam: Comparative studies of legal systems: Preliminary results. Paper presented at the Seventh World Congress of Sociology, Varna, 1970, (Stencil). See also preceeding paper.

Reckless, Walter C.: The development of a Criminality Level Index: In: Walter C. Reckless & Charles L. Newman: *Interdisciplinary problems in criminology: Papers of the American Society of Criminology, 1964.* Columbus, Ohio: The Ohio State University, 1965. pp. 71–82.

Reckless, W. C. & Ferracuti, F.: Atteggiamenti verso la legge, i tribunali e la polizia: contronto tra adulti criminali e non criminali (attitudes towards law, courts and police: a comparison of adult criminals and non criminals). *Quad Criminol. clin.* 1968, *10,* (3), 275–290. (Abstract.)

Rose, Arnold M. & Prell, Arthur E.: Does the punishment fit the crime? A study in social valuation. *American Journal of Sociology,* 1955, *61,* 247–259.

Savigny, Freidrich Karl von: *Vom Beruf unsere Zeit für Gesetzgebung und Rechtswissenschaft.* Heidelberg, 1814.

Schmidt, F., Gräntze, L. & Ross, A.: *Arbetstid och semester för jordbrukets utearbetare.* Lund: Gleerup, 1946.

Schuyt, Cess, J. M. & Ruys, Joop C. M.: Attitudes towards new socio-economic legislation: A before–after study of the normative effects of the introduction of tax on added value (TAV). Leiden, Holland: Faculty of Law, State University of Leiden, 1971. (Stencil).

Sechrest, Dale K.: Comparisons of inmates' and staff's judgements of the severity of offences. *Journal of Research in Crime and Delinquency,* 1969, *6,* 41–55.

Segerstedt, T., Karlsson, G. & Rundblad, B.: A research into the general sense of justice. *Theoria,* 1949, *15,* 321–338.

Shoham, Shlomo & Shaskolsky, Leon: An analysis of delinquents and non-delinquents in Israel: A cross-cultural perspective. *Sociology and Social Research,* 1969, *53,* 333–343.

Simpson, Ray Mars: Attitudes of teachers and prisoners towards the seriousness of criminal acts. *Journal of Criminal Law, Criminology and Police Science,* 1934–35, *25,* 76–83.

Stjernquist, Per: How are changes in social behaviour developed by means of legislation? In: *Legal essays. A tribute to Frede Castberg.* Oslo: Universitetsforlaget, 1963. pp. 153–169.

Sumner, W. G.: *Folkways,* Boston: Ginn & Co. 1906.

Sutherland, Edwin H. & Cressey, Donald R.: *Principles of criminology.* Chicago: Lippincott, 1960.

Sykes, Gresham M. & Matza, David: Techniques of neutralisation: A theory of delinquency. *American Sociological Review,* 1957, *22,* 664–670.

Syrén, S. & Tham, H.: Brottslighet, normer och sanktioner (Delinquency, norms, and sanctions). Uppsala Universitetet, Sociologiska Institutionen, 1968. (Stencil).

Tarde, G.: *Les lois de l'imitation, Etude sociologique,* Paris, 1890.

Thurstone, L. L.: The method of paired comparisons for social values. *Journal of Abnormal and Social Psychology,* 1927, *21,* 384–400.

Thurstone, L. L.: Influence of motion pictures on children's attitudes. *Journal of Social Psychology,* 1931, 291–305.

Toro-Calder, Jaime, Cedeño, Ceferina & Reckless, Walter C.: A comparative study of Puerto Rican attitudes toward the legal system dealing with crime. *The Journal of Criminal Law, Criminology and Police Science,* 1968, *58,* 536–541.

Waldo, Gordon P. & Hall, Nason E.: Delinquency potential and attitudes toward the criminal justice system. *Social Forces,* 1970, *49,* 291–298.

Walker, N. & Argyle, M.: Does the law affect moral judgements? *British Journal of Criminology,* 1964, *4,* 570–581.

van Houtte, J.: Paper presented at 7th World Congress of Sociology. By Lafaille, R., Lefevre, J. & van Houtte, J. Varna, 1970 (Stencil).

Versele, S. C. (Ed.): Projet de rapport sur le sondage d'opinion KOL Groupe de contact 'juristes—sociologues'. Université Libre de Bruxelles, Institut de Sociologie, Centre de Sociologie du Droit et de la Justice, 1971. (Stencil).

Wolfenden, John: *Report of the Committee on Homosexual Offences and Prostitution.* London: Command 247, 1957.